STUDY GUIDE
HENRY BORNE
Holy Cross College

MARRIAGES AND FAMILIES
Diversity and Change

THIRD EDITION

Mary Ann Schwartz
Northeastern Illinois University

BarBara Marliene Scott
Northeastern Illinois University

ISBN 0-13-013593-3

Printed in the United States of America

Table of Contents

Preface

This Study Guide has been written to enhance the foundation of sociological ideas and issues that are presented in the text, *Marriages and Families* by Mary Ann Schwartz and Barbara Marliene Scott. To help you review and think about the material found in the text, the Study Guide has been organized into several different sections to accompany each chapter in the text.

A ***Chapter Outline*** provides a basis for organizing segments of information from each chapter in the text. A section on ***Learning Objectives*** identifies the basic knowledge, explanations, comparisons, and understandings students should have after reading and reflecting upon each chapter. This section is followed by a section entitled **Key Terms** in which the important concepts from each chapter are listed, with space provided for the student to write out the definition for each of the terms. This section is followed by the ***Important Researchers*** section. Many of the researchers cited in the text are listed, with space provided for students to write out important ideas, findings, etc. for each research. The next section provides ***Study Questions***, including true-false, multiple-choice, matching, fill-in, and short answer type questions. The following section provides the ***Answers to Study Questions***, including a list of the page numbers where the answers to these questions can be found. The seventh section, ***In Focus—Important Issues***, provides the student an opportunity to answer questions relating to some of the more important concepts and ideas presented in each chapter. The final section, ***Analysis and Comment***, provides space for students to raise questions and make comments on the boxes in each chapter.

This Study Guide is intended to a learning tool to accompany the text *Marriages and Families*. It will hopefully provide the student with opportunities to more deeply benefit from the knowledge of sociology which the authors offer concerning marriage and family life.

On a personal note I want to congratulate Dr. Schwartz and Dr. Scott for writing such an excellent and engaging text on marriages and families. They offer students a very meaningful perspective on many important issues in marriage and family life. I believe students will be excited by this text, and rewarded by what it has to offer them both personally and academically. It has been a pleasure for me to write this Study Guide. I would like to thank Sharon Chambliss, Managing Editor, Sociology of Prentice Hall for her insight, guidance, and support. It is a joy working for people such as her. I appreciate this opportunity given to me. Finally, my love to my family—Cincy, Ben, and Abby—for their support and love.

HB

1 Marriages and Families Over Time

PART I: CHAPTER OUTLINE

I.   Contemporary Definitions of Marriages and Families
    A.   What is a Marriage?
    B.   What is a Family?
    C.   Race, Class, and Gender
II.   Family Functions and the Debate Over Family Values
    A.   Social Functions of Families
    B.   Contrasting Views of Families
III.   Debunking Myths About Marriages and Families
    A.   Myth 1: The Universal Nuclear Family
    B.   Myth 2: The Self-Reliant Traditional Family
    C.   Myth 3: The Naturalness of Different Spheres for Wives and Husbands
    D.   Myth 4: The Unstable African American Family
    E.   Myth 5: The Idealized Nuclear Family of the 1950s
IV.   Families In Early America
    A.   Colonial Families
    B.   African American Families under Slavery
    C.   Free African American Families
    D.   Slavery's Hidden Legacy: Racial Mixing
    E.   Native American Families
V.   Families In the Nineteenth Century
    A.   Emergence of the Good Provider Role
    B.   The Cult of Domesticity
    C.   Changing Views of Childhood
    D.   The Impact of Class and Ethnicity
    E.   Immigration and Family Life
    F.   The Economic Roles of Women and Children
    G.   Ethnic and Racial Family Patterns
    H.   Mexican American Families
VI.   Families In the Early Twentieth Century
    A.   The Emergence of the Companionate Family
    B.   The Great Depression
    C.   World War II and Its Aftermath
    D.   New Immigration in the Latter Half of the Twentieth Century
    E.   Lessons from History
VII.   Contemporary Patterns In Marriages and Families
VIII.   Looking Ahead: Marriages and Families In the Future

IX.   The Sociological Imagination
X.   Writing Your Own Script
XI.   Summary
XII.   Key Terms
XIII.   Questions for Study and Reflection
XIV.   Further Reading

PART II: LEARNING OBJECTIVES

1. To recognize the diversity of marriage and family forms existing in the United States and around the world.
2. To develop broader and more socially relevant definitions for the institutions of marriage and family.
3. To recognize the important social functions served by the institution of the family.
4. To discuss contrasting views of families and how these relate to important cultural values in society.
5. To critically assess one's assumptions about the social institutions of marriage and the family, and in so doing debunk myths about them.
6. To develop a historical understanding of marriages and families in the United States, including the experiences of African Americans, Native Americans, Mexican Americans, and European immigrants.
7. To consider issues relating to race, gender, social class, and age as they have affected family experiences during the nineteenth and twentieth centuries.
8. To review important historical events that occurred during the twentieth century that have helped shape family life in the United States.
9. To develop a sense of the sociological imagination and begin to recognize the benefits such a perspective can have in our personal lives.
10. To begin to systematically evaluate your feelings and desires regarding the life choices you have made or will be making over the course of your lifetime.

PART III: KEY TERMS

Define each of the following terms in the space provided or on separate paper. Check the accuracy of your answers by referring to the text. Do the same for each chapter in the text as each is assigned in class.

cenogamy

companionate family

coverature

family

extended family

familism

family of orientation

family of procreation

household

institution

institutional racism

kinship

marriage

matrilineal

modified extended family

monogamy

myth

nuclear family

patriarchal family

patrilineal

polyandry

polygamy

polygyny

role

serial monogamy

socialization

social structure

sociological imagination

status

PART IV: IMPORTANT RESEARCHERS

Go back through the chapter and find references to the following people and their work on marriages and families. In the space provided below briefly write down key points about each person's work. Also, jot down any questions or comments you may have about the research presented. These people and their work may be mentioned more than once in the chapter. Be prepared to discuss your comments and questions in class.

Jesse Bernard   Andrew Billingsly

Stephanie Coontz   John Demos

Christopher Lasch   C. Wright Mills

Steven Mintz and Susan Kellog

PART V: STUDY QUESTIONS

True-False

1.   Our authors suggest that we need to develop a more *narrow and precise* definition of *marriage* than is currently being used in our society.   T F
2.   The *family of orientation* is the family into which a person is born and raised.   T F
3.   Our authors suggest that the *family mosaic* in the United States is limited primarily to *nuclear* and *extended families*.   T F
4.   *Modified extended families* may not include a marriage, but always includes at least three or more generations living in the same household.   T F
5.   Every known society has some form of *incest taboo*.   T F
6.   Although the United States has one of the highest *divorce rates* in the world, the overwhelming majority of divorced people eventually *remarry*.   T F
7.   A 1993 government survey in *India* found that over half of the females in the Northern States marry before reaching fifteen years of age.   T F
8.   Our authors define *myth* as a false, fictitious, imaginary, or exaggerated belief about someone or something.   T F

9. The *median age at first marriage* in the U.S. has been consistently rising decade by decade during the twentieth century. T F
10. As compared to the 1990s, the 1950s were characterized by younger ages at marriage, higher birth rates, and lower divorce and premarital pregnancy rates. T F
11. Most people in *colonial America* lived in *extended families*. T F
12. Most *freed slaves* prior to the Civil War lived in the *North*. T F
13. Industrialization advanced the *ideology of domesticity* for women. T F
14. During the nineteenth century, the *cult of domesticity* for women was the counterpart to the *good provider role* for males. T F
15. The economic transformation that took place in the early nineteenth century in our society altered children's roles, providing a context in which *childhood* was seen as a separate period in the life course. T F
16. Women and children in families of the early nineteenth century contributed very little to the *material support* of their families. T F
17. World War II brought about numerous changes in families—primary among them being the dramatic increase in the *marriage rate*. T F
18. In 1997 most families in the U.S. were comprised of *married couples with children*. T F

Multiple-Choice

1. Our authors use a very comprehensive and reality-based definition for _____, or a union between people (whether widely or legally recognized or not) that unites partners sexually, socially, and economically; that is relatively consistent over time; and that accords each member certain agreed-upon rights.

    (a)   marriage
    (b)   family
    (c)   kinship
    (d)   community
    (e)   society

2. *Cenogamy* refers to:

    (a)   sibling marriages.
    (b)   group marriage.
    (c)   same-sex marriage.
    (d)   one woman being married to two or more men.

3. A *surrogate family* is also known as a _____ family.

    (a)   multigenerational
    (b)   patriarchal
    (c)   reconstituted
    (d)   blended
    (e)   chosen

4. A family in which the male (husband or father) is the head of the family and exercises authority and decision-making power over his wife and child(ren) is termed:

    (a) the extended family.
    (b) the affinal family.
    (c) the nuclear family.
    (d) the patriarchal family.
    (e) the consanguine family.

5. _____ are cultural guidelines or rules.

    (a) Statuses
    (b) Norms
    (c) Institutions
    (d) Roles
    (e) Myths

6. The _____ of society refers to the recurrent patterned ways that people relate to one another.

    (a) social structure
    (b) norm structure
    (c) cultural structure
    (d) organizational structure

7. Which of the following *is not identified* by the authors as *myths* or *stereotypes* about the family?

    (a) the naturalness of different spheres for wives and husbands
    (b) the private and autonomous family
    (c) the unstable African American family
    (d) the dependent traditional family
    (e) the idealized nuclear family of the 1950s

8. Andrew Billingsly's research on African American families during the 1960s identified ____ *percent* as represented a lower class made up of stable working-class families and both stable and multi-problem poor families.

    (a) 10
    (b) 50
    (c) 40
    (d) 60
    (e) 30

9. According to our authors, which of the following statements characterizes *colonial families* in America?

   (a) The nuclear family structure was the dominate form.
   (b) The family formed the basic economic unit of society.
   (c) Functions of the family were interwoven within the larger community.
   (d) All of the above.
   (e) None of the above.

10. The English concept of *coverture* related to:

    (a) assimilation of African Americans into white society after the Civil War.
    (b) nonfamily household servants during America's colonial period.
    (c) a wife's legal identity.
    (d) the working status of young children in colonial America.

11. Andrew Billingsly points out which of the following concerning *African American families under slavery*?

    (a) Unlike most of their colonial contemporaries, African Americans came to America from Africa and not from Europe.
    (b) They were uprooted from their cultural and family moorings and brought to the United States as slaves.
    (c) From the beginning and continuing even today, they were systematically excluded from participation in the major institutions of U.S. society.
    (d) All of the above.
    (e) None of the above.

12. The basic social unit of *Iroquois* society during America's colonial period was the:

    (a) patriarchal family.
    (b) principle of coverture.
    (c) blended family.
    (d) reconstituted family.
    (e) longhouse.

13. According to sociologist Jessie Bernard, a specialized role known as the _____ *role* emerged around 1830. The essence of this role was that a man's major contribution to his family is economic.

    (a) affective
    (b) expressive
    (c) good provider
    (d) domestic cult
    (e) companionate

14. The first wave of *immigrants* to the U.S. during the middle of the ninetheenth century were predominately from:

   (a) Southern Europe.
   (b) Eastern Europe.
   (c) Northern and Western Europe.
   (d) the Middle-East.

15. Several points are being made in the text concerning the economic role of women and children during the nineteenth century, including:

   (a) overall, a working-class wife did not work outside the home unless her spouse lost his job or was unable to work because of illness or injury.
   (b) wives often supplemented family income by taking in boarders, or by doing laundry or sewing in their homes.
   (c) working outside the home was more common among first-generation immigrant women whose husbands earned less than their native-born counterparts.
   (d) all of the above.
   (e) none of the above.

16. One of the most distinctive features of the *Chicano family* of the early nineteenth century was the emphasis on:

   (a) familism.
   (b) isolationism.
   (c) cenogamy.
   (d) the isolated nuclear family.

17. The *companionate family* emerged in the United States:

   (a) during the early colonial period.
   (b) just prior to the Civil War.
   (c) after World War II.
   (d) during the early twentieth century.
   (e) during the 1970s.

18. The impact of the *Great Depression* on young adults and families included:

   (a) delaying marriage.
   (b) couples postponing having children.
   (c) an increase in desertion.
   (d) all of the above.
   (e) none of the above.

19. Which of the following is identified in the text as a *lesson of history* we should learn?

   (a) Changes in family life will likely not be very significant during the next generation as compared to the previous generation or two.
   (b) Although families have changed continuously over time, this change has not been in any single direction.
   (c) Keeping a sense of a family nostalgia will help create a context in which policies and programs can more effectively help current families adapt.
   (d) None of the above.
   (e) Choices a, b, and c are all accurate .

20. What percentage of U.S. *households* in 1997 were classified as *nonfamilies*?

   (a) 20
   (b) 10
   (c) 40
   (d) 60
   (e) 30

21. The *sociological imagination* most immediately involves:

   (a) understanding how individuals determine their own destinies.
   (b) grasping history and biography and the relations between the two within our society.
   (c) perceiving social interaction in families as being principally constructed by the tradition.
   (d) recognizing the commonly held social experiences of all members of society.

Matching

a.	cult of domesticity	n.	institutional racism
b.	role	o.	polyandry
c.	norms	p.	household
d.	social structure	q.	foster family
e.	polygamy	r.	marriage
f.	institution	s.	matriarchy
g.	the sociological imagination	t.	status
h.	causality	u.	extended family
i.	surrogate family	v.	kinship
j.	matrilineal descent	w.	family of orientation
k.	cenogamy	x.	theory
l.	sanctions	y.	methods
m.	companionate family	z.	home

1. Cultural guidelines or rules of conduct that direct people to behave in particular ways. _____ .

2. The family into which one is born. _____

3. A marriage structure or category referring to one person of one sex married to several people of the other sex. ____

4. A union between people that unites partners sexually, socially, and economically; that is relatively consistent over time; and that accords each member certain agreed upon rights. ____

5. Patterns of ideas, beliefs, values, and behavior that are built around basic needs of individuals and society and that tend to persist over time. ____

6. Group marriage. ____

7. A marriage type in which one wife has two or more husbands. ____

8. A position in a group or society. ____

9. All persons who occupy a housing unit. ____

10. Grasping history and biography and the relations between the two within our society. ____

11. The systematic discrimination against a racial group by the institutions within a society and structural shifts in the economy and related trends that have created new and deeper disparities in the structure and quality of family life between blacks and whites in society. ____

12. The recurrent, patterned ways that people relate to one another. ____

13. The counterpart to the good provider role. ____

14. People who are related by blood, marriage, or adoption, or who consider one another family. ____

15. A set of behaviors associated with a particular status. ____

16. Whereby kinship of family lineage (descent) and inheritance come through the mother and her blood relatives. ____

17. A set of "roommates," or group of people either of different or the same sex who choose to share the same household and who define themselves as a family. ____

18. A twentieth century model for heterosexual relationships based on mutual affection, sexual fulfillment, and sharing domestic tasks and child rearing. ____

Fill-In

1. In 1998, Kanwar Ahson of Karachi, Pakistan was arrested to face charges of having sex outside of marriage. What makes this story noteworthy is that Riffat Afrdie, the woman Kanwar had sex with, was his _____.

2. _____ is a broad category that refers generally to one person of one sex married to several people of the other sex.

3. *Polygamy* can take two forms, _____, in which one male has two or more wives, and _____ in which one female has two of more husbands.

4. _____ is the legally recognized marriage structure in the U.S. However, because approximately one-half of all marriages end in divorce and the vast majority of divorced people remarry, the U.S. marriage pattern is more accurately classified as

_____.

5. The *family of* _____ is the family into which a person is born and raised.

6. Three of the most important *social categories* of experience for individuals and families in the U.S., primarily because these categories also represent significant, comprehensive, and structured systems of oppression for some individuals and groups and privilege for others, are _____, _____, and _____.

7. Several *social functions* of the family are identified and illustrated in the text, including: _____ of sexual behavior, _____, social _____, _____, economic _____, and care, protection, and _____.

8. *Christopher Lasch* contends that the encroachment of outside institutions, especially the state, has left modern families with too few _____.

9. A _____ is a false, fictitious, imaginary, or exaggerated belief about someone or something.

10. Public opinion polls during the 1950s found that ___ *percent* of couples considered themselves in *unhappy marriages*.

11. In *colonial America*, the _____ formed the basic economic unit.

12. The *colonial family* was a _____. Fathers were regarded as the head of the family, and exercised authority over wives, children, and servants.

13. Regarding extended kinship patterns, strong kinship feelings among *slaves* are evident from the _____ practices of slave families.

14. Northeastern woodlands peoples, prior to European arrival, lived in diverse cultures. The social and economic unit of the *Algonquins* was the _____, whereas for the *Iroquois* it was the _____.

15. One of the *rules of descent* is called _____, whereby kinship or family lineage and inheritance come through the father and his blood relatives. Another is called _____, whereby kinship or family lineage and inheritance come through the mother and her blood relatives.

16. According to sociologist *Jessie Bernard,* a specialized male role emerged in the U.S. around 1839. She labeled this the _____ *role*.

17. In 1900 approximately _____ *percent* of black women were in the labor force, compared to _____ *percent* of white women.

18. The traditional male role in the nineteenth century *Chicano household* was referred to as _____.

19. During the early twentieth century the idea of a more personal and _____ model for heterosexual relationships based on mutual affection, sexual fulfillment, and sharing of domestic tasks and child rearing emerged.

20. Our authors identify several *lessons from history*. These include: (1) Although families have changed continuously over time, this change has not been in any _____ direction. (2) We cannot say with any _____ which changes have been good or bad. (3) Throughout history there has never been a _____ family form. (4) Understanding the source of our _____ view of the "traditional" family can lead us to develop a more realistic sense of families. and (5) Given the past, it is likely that additional changes in family life will _____.

21. In 1997, _____ *percent* of families in the U.S. were composed of a *married couple with children*. In 1970 this percentage was _____.

22. The _____ refers to the grasping of history and biography and the relations between the two within our society.

Short-Answer

1. How is *marriage* typically defined in our society? What concerns do our authors have about such a definition? What definition are they proposing we use?

2.	What is the connection between *power relationships* and the definition of the family? How does the definition of the family relate to *family policy issues*? Can you provide an example to illustrate this connection?
3.	Identify and define five family arrangements (structures) other than the traditional nuclear family.
4.	What are the six *social functions of the family*? Provide an illustration for each of these.
5.	Provide three pieces of evidence from our society's history that support *Stephanie Coontz's* argument that we have and *idealized* vision of the past that never actually existed.
6.	What historical factors can you think of that may have influenced the *median age at first marriage* in the U.S. over the last century. Please refer to *Figure 1.1* (p. 12).
7.	*Andrew Billingsly* points out three important elements that distinguish the experiences of African Americans from that of other groups in the United States. What are these elements? To what extent do you agree with his conclusions?
8.	What are the major characteristics of the *companionate family?*
9.	What do sociologists *Margaret Andersen* and *Patricia Hill Collins* mean when they say they have observed race, class, and gender as key parts of the total fabric of experience of all families? What illustrations can you provide in support of their view?
10.	What are the kinds of questions about society using the *sociological imagination?* What are four benefits of this perspective?
11.	What do the authors mean by *writing your own script?*

PART VI: ANSWERS TO STUDY QUESTIONS

True-False

1.	F	(p. 2)	10.	T	(p. 12)
2.	T	(p. 3)	11.	F	(p. 14)
3.	F	(p. 3)	12.	F	(p. 17)
4.	F	(p. 3)	13.	T	(p. 20)
5.	T	(p. 3)	14.	T	(p. 20)
6.	T	(p. 5)	15.	T	(p. 20)
7.	T	(p. 6)	16.	F	(p. 21)
8.	T	(p. 9)	17.	T	(p. 23)
9.	F	(p. 12)	18.	F	(p. 23)

Multiple-Choice

1.	a	(p. 2)	12.	e	(p. 16)
2.	b	(p. 2)	13.	c	(p. 19)
3.	e	(p. 3)	14.	c	(p. 20)
4.	d	(p. 4)	15.	d	(p. 21)
5.	b	(p. 5)	16.	a	(p. 22)
6.	a	(p. 5)	17.	d	(p. 22)
7.	d	(pp. 9-12)	18.	d	(p. 23)
8.	b	(p. 11)	19.	b	(pp. 24-25)
9.	d	(p. 14)	20.	e	(p. 25)
10.	c	(p. 15)	21.	b	(p. 26)
11.	d	(p. 18)			

Matching

1.	c	(p. 5)	10.	g	(p. 26)
2.	w	(p. 3)	11.	n	(p. 12)
3.	e	(p. 2)	12.	d	(p. 5)
4.	r	(p. 2)	13.	a	(p. 20)
5.	f	(p. 2)	14.	v	(p. 14)
6.	k	(p. 2)	15.	b	(p. 5)
7.	o	(p. 2)	16.	j	(pp. 18-19)
8.	t	(p. 5)	17.	i	(p. 3)
9.	p	(p. 25)	18.	m	(p. 22)
10.	g	(p. 26)			

Fill-In

1.   wife (p. 1)
2.   Polygamy (p. 2)
3.   polygyny, polyandry (p. 2)
2.   monogamy, serial monogamy (p. 2)
3.   orientation (p. 3)
4.   race, class, gender (p. 4)
5.   regulation, reproduction, placement, socialization, cooperation, intimacy (pp. 5-7)
6.   functions (p. 7)
7.   myth (p. 9)
8.   20 (p. 13)
9.   family (p. 14)
10. patriarchy (p. 15)
11. naming (p. 17)
12. wigwam, longhouse (p. 18)
13. patrilineal, matrilineal (pp. 18-19)
14. good provider (p. 19)
15. 41, 16 (p. 21)
16. machismo (p. 22)
17. companionate (p. 22)
18. single, certainty, perfect, idealized, continue (pp. 24-25)
19. 25, 40 (p. 25)
20. sociological imagination (p. 26)

PART VII: IN FOCUS--MAJOR ISSUES

- Contemporary Definitions of Marriages and Families

What are the three general *marriage types* identified in the text?

• Identify and provide an illustration for five of the *types of families* identified in the text:

• Family Functions and the Debate Over Family Values

Provide an illustration for each of the following *social functions of the family*:

regulation of sexual behavior   social placement

reproduction   socialization

economic cooperation   care, protection, and intimacy

Describe the two *contrasting views of families* identified in the text:

• Debunking Myths about Marriages and Families

According to the authors, what traits do people usually use to describe the *traditional family*?

What evidence is being provided in the text to suggest these traits are inaccurate?

- Families in Early America

  Identify one important point made by the authors for each of the following:

  Colonial families

  African American families under slavery

  Native American families

- Families in the Nineteenth Century

  What was the *good provider role?*

  What was the *cult of domesticity*?

  Describe in a few sentences how the views of *childhood* changed in the early part of the nineteenth century.

- Families in the Early Twentieth Century

  What is meant by the *companionate family*?

  What are three important historical events identified by the authors that dramatically affected families during the twentieth century? Illustrate two of these.

- Contemporary Patterns

  What are the five *lessons of history* identified by our authors?

- The Sociological Imagination

  Define and provide an illustration for this perspective:

PART VIII: ANALYSIS AND COMMENT

- In Other Places: Child Marriages in India (p. 6)

  Key Points: Comments/Questions:

- Strengthening Marriages and Families (p. 10)

  Key Points: Comments/Questions:

- Writing Your Own Script: Define It, and Knowledge Follows (p. 28)

  Key Points: Comments/Questions:

2 Ways of Studying and Explaining Marriages and Families

PART I: CHAPTER OUTLINE

I.   The Sociology of Marriages and Families
II.   Studying Marriages and Families: The Link Between Research and Theory
III.   Methodological Techniques in the Study of Marriages and Families
     A.   Surveys
     B.   Observation
     C.   Case Studies
     D.   Ethnography
     E.   Scientific Methodologies Used by Feminist Researchers
IV.   A Critical Look at Traditional Research on Marriages and Families
     A.   Who Does and Does Not Get Studied
     B.   The Need for a New Scholarship on Marriages and Families
V.   Theoretical Perspectives
     A.   Structural Functionalism
     B.   Conflict Theory
     C.   Symbolic Interactionism
     D.   Social Constructionism
     E.   Social Exchange Theory
     F.   The Developmental Family Life Cycle Model
     G.   Feminist Theory
VI.   Men's Studies Relative to Marriages and Families
     A.   Men in Families
VII.   Summary
VIII.   Key Terms
IX.   Questions for Study and Reflection
X.   Further Reading

PART II: LEARNING OBJECTIVES

1. To begin to develop an appreciation of how the sociological perspective can help us better understand issues relating to marriages and families.
2. To begin to develop an understanding about the relationship between theory and research in the study of marriages and families.
3. To gain basic knowledge about the scientific method, including the major research techniques used by social scientists for the study of marriages and families.

4.   To recognize the biases in social science research in terms of stereotypical approaches to the study of women, lower-class families, and racial and ethnic minorities.

5.   To become aware of the need for new scholarship on marriages and families, and to begin to think about alternatives to traditional research methods typically used for the study of white, middle-class families.

6.   To be able to identify and describe the major theoretical perspectives used by sociologists for the study of marriages and families.

7.   To become aware of gender issues related to research on marriages and families.

PART III: KEY TERMS

case study

conflict theory

developmental family life cycle theory

dysfunctional

empirical research

ethnography

expressive traits

feminism

functional

Hawthorne effect

hypothesis

ideologies

instrumental traits

interview

manifest functions

qualitative methods

quantitative methods

questionnaire

reliability

scientific method

scientific research

sexism

social constructionism

social construction of reality

social-exchange theory

survey

symbolic interactionism

symbols

theory

theory model

validity

variables

   dependent variable

   independent variable

PART IV: IMPORTANT RESEARCHERS

Ellen Annandale   Jessie Bernard

Peter Blau and Otis Duncan   Phillip Blumstein and Pepper Schwartz

Bruce Brown and Tony McCormick   Emile Durkheim

Evelyn Duvall   Paul Glick

George Homans and Peter Blau   Robin Jarrett

Karl Marx   Tony McCormick

Daniel Moynihan   Talcott Parsons

Barbara Scott

PART V: STUDY QUESTIONS

True-False

1. In 1997, the American Medical Association was the number one spender on lobbying among organizations seeking to influence lawmakers. T F
2. *Theories* relate ideas and observations to each other as well as help explain them. T F
3. In scientific research, the term *independent variable* is used to identify a cause—it is a variable that causes change in or affects another variable. T F
4. A potential problem for all scientific research is a lack of *objectivity*. T F
5. The *survey* is the most widely used research method sociologists employ for the study of marriages and families. T F
6. *Reliability* refers to the degree to which a study measures exactly what it claims to be measuring. T F
7. *Qualitative methods* are designed to study variables that can be measured numerically. T F
8. *Ethnographies* tend to produce more reliable, valid, and objective data than any other research method. T F
9. *Ideologies* are systems of belief. T F
10. More is known from survey data about gay and lesbian couples than is known about African American couples or poor couples. T F
11. Basically, *structural functionalism* views society as an organized and stable system, analogous to the human system, that is made up of a variety of interrelated parts or structures. T F
12. *Talcott Parsons*, a structural functionalist, argued that in modern society the functional importance of the nuclear family has declined as many of its functions have been taken over and performed by other social institutions. T F
13. *Instrumental traits* encourage nurturance, emotionality, sensitivity, and warmth. T F
14. According to *conflict theorists*, conflict is natural and inevitable in all human interaction, including family life. T F
15. *Symbolic interactionism* tends to focus on *macropatterns* that characterize society. T F
16. *Social constructionism* is an extension of structural functionalism. T F

20

17. According to social constructionist thinking, the important facts of human social life are not inherent in human biology but are developed through a complex process of human interaction. T F
18. *Exchange theorists* assume that humans are rational beings. T F
19. Our authors suggest *feminist theory*, unlike other theories discussed in the text, has a single, unified view. T F
20. One very important criticism of most feminist theories is that they are biased toward the experiences of white, middle-class, heterosexual women. T F

Multiple-Choice

1. Statements of relationships between two or more variables are called:

    (a)   science.
    (b)   reliability.
    (c)   validity.
    (d)   hypotheses.
    (e)   research methods.

2. Which of the following statements about theories is *not* accurate?

    (a)   A theory is an explanation of some phenomenon.
    (b)   Theories relate ideas and observations to each other.
    (c)   Theories make certain assumptions about the world.
    (d)   Theories do not include unstated or states value judgements.

3. *Scientific research* provides us with _____ *evidence* as a basis for knowledge or theories.

    (a)   ideological
    (b)   real
    (c)   empirical
    (d)   subjective
    (e)   truthful

4. The degree to which a study *measures exactly what it claims to be measuring* is known as:

    (a)   validity.
    (b)   consistency.
    (c)   ethnography.
    (d)   reliability.

5. What is the most widely used method for studying marriages and families?

    (a)   cases studies
    (b)   experiments
    (c)   participant observation
    (d)   ethnographies
    (e)   surveys

6.   The two basic methods by which researchers ask questions using surveys include:

(a)   experiments and participant observation.
(b)   case studies and ethnographies.
(c)   interviews and questionnaires.
(d)   secondary analysis and fieldwork.

7.   When a researcher becomes a member of the group she or he is studying this is known as:

(a)   researcher bias
(b)   the Hawthorne effect
(c)   participant observation
(d)   quantitative research
(e)   validity

8.   When people become aware that they are being studied they frequently modify their behavior. This is known as:

(a)   subject bias.
(b)   participant bas.
(c)   the reliability crisis.
(d)   the Hawthorne effect.
(e)   validity crisis.

9.   *Bruce Brown* and *Tony McCormick* conducted a case study of six families in which one member had:

(a)   died.
(b)   suffered a head injury.
(c)   been born blind.
(d)   became pregnant
(e)   been a drug addict.

10.   An interesting example of ethnographic research undertaken by *Robbin Jarrett* who focused on:

(a)   low-income African American families.
(b)   gay couples.
(c)   white working-class families.
(d)   single parent families.

11.   *Feminist researchers* are concerned with:

(a)   who researchers study.
(b)   how researchers study people.
(c)   how researchers draw conclusions.
(d)   what evidence conclusions are drawn on.
(e)   all of the above.

12. A major weakness of most research on *occupational mobility* in the United States, as evidenced by a study done by *Peter Blau and Otis Duncan*, has been:

    (a) a focus on whites.
    (b) a focus on the very wealthy.
    (c) a focus on families and not individuals.
    (d) a focus on men and not women.

13. The *Moynihan Report* of 1965 focused on:

    (a) African American families.
    (b) homosexual marriages.
    (c) education and social mobility.
    (d) religious practices and family solidarity.
    (e) cohabitation and marital stability.

14. Which of the following theories views society as an organized, stable system, analogous to the human system, that is made up of a variety of interrelated parts?

    (a) humanism
    (b) structural functionalism
    (c) social conflict
    (d) social contructionism
    (e) symbolic interactionism

15. Structural functionalists identify two types of *functions*—recognized and intended and unintended and unrecognized. These are referred to as:

    (a) basic and secondary.
    (b) ordered and strained.
    (c) manifest and latent.
    (d) primary and residual.

16. According to structural functionalist *Talcott Parsons*, the two major functions of the modern nuclear family are:

    (a) recreation and retreat.
    (b) economic stability and affection.
    (c) socialization of the young and personality stabilization of adults.
    (d) procreation and education.

17. _____ *theorists* focus on society as an arena where individuals and groups compete over limited resources.

    (a) Symbolic interactionist
    (b) Structural functionalist
    (c) Conflict
    (d) Social-exchange
    (e) Social constructionist

18.   Which of the following is/are *criticisms of conflict theory*?

(a)   The underlying assumption is that power is people's main objective.
(b)   That conflict is the major feature of social life is too narrow a view.
(c)   They explicitly advocate social change.
(d)   Value neutrality may not be being maintained in research.
(e)   All of the above.

19.   *Jessie Bernard's* perspective that men and women are likely to view and experience their marriages differently—referring to this phenomenon as "his" and "her" marriages, is derived from _____ theory.

(a)   structural functionalism
(b)   conflict
(c)   feminist
(d)   symbolic interaction

20.   Which of the following theories is also known as the *rational-choice perspective*?

(a)   social conflict
(b)   structural functionalism
(c)   symbolic interactionism
(d)   social constructionist
(e)   social-exchange

21.   Which of the following theories most directly focuses attention on the stages in the family life cycle?

(a)   developmental family life cycle
(b)   social exchange
(c)   structural functionalism
(d)   symbolic interactionism
(e)   social conflict

22.   To be considered *feminist*, research must be committed to activist goals. In addition, it should adopt which of the following basic philosophical approaches?

(a)   Gender is the central focus of the research.
(b)   Status quo gender relations are to be viewed as problematic in that women are defined as subordinate to men.
(c)   Gender relations are to be viewed as the result of social, not natural, factors.
(d)   All of the above.

Matching

a.	expressive traits	i.	case study
b.	reliability	j.	structural functionalism
c.	instrumental traits	k.	developmental family life cycle model
d.	questionnaire	l.	social interactionism
e.	scientific method	m.	perspective
f.	latent functions	n.	conflict theory
g.	social-exchange theory	o.	symbols
h.	theory	p.	the social construction of reality

1. Focuses on micropatterns of face-to-face interaction among people in specific settings. _____

2. Unintended or unrecognized consequences. _____

3. Objects, words, sounds, and events that are given meaning by members of a culture—and construct reality as they go about the business of their daily lives. _____

4. An explanation of some phenomenon—relating ideas and observations, and containing certain assumptions about the world, the nature of society and human behavior. _____

5. View society as an organized and stable system, analogous to the human system, that is made up of a variety of interrelated parts or structures. _____

6. Encourage self-confidence, rationality, competition, and coolness. _____

7. Also known as the rational-choice perspective because of its focus on costs, benefits, and the expectation of reciprocity. _____

8. A set of procedures intended to ensure accuracy and honesty throughout the research process. _____

9. A detailed and in-depth examination of a single unit. _____

10. The process whereby people assign meanings to social phenomena. _____

11. Pays close attention to families over time and attempts to explain family life in terms of a process. _____

12. Encourages nurturance, emotionality, sensitivity, and warmth. _____

13. Central themes include—humans have basic interests or things they want to acquire; power is the basis of all relationships, and is scarce and unequally distributed and coercive; and values and ideas are weapons used by different groups to advance their own needs. _____

14. The degree to which the research yields the same results when repeated by the same researcher or other researchers. _____

15. A research technique for describing a group from the group's point of view. _____

16. A type of survey involving a set of printed questions that people read on their own and record the answers. _____

Fill-In

1. A _____ is an explanation of some phenomenon.

2. By _____ *evidence* we mean data or evidence that can be confirmed by the use of one or more of the human senses.

3. All *scientific research* is guided by the _____, or a set of procedures intended to ensure accuracy and honesty throughout the research process.

4. _____ is the degree to which the research yields the same results when repeated by the same researcher or other researchers.

5. The two basic methods by which researchers ask questions and receive answers using *surveys* are _____ and _____.

6. In general, _____ is a research technique for describing a social group from the group's point of view.

7. _____ *methods* are designed to study variables that can be measured numerically. _____ m*ethods* are designed to study conditions or processes that are hard to measure numerically.

8. According to researchers *Peter Blau* and *Otis Duncan*, social mobility was simply a function of _____ and _____ and that no other conditions affect changes for social mobility in the United States.

9. Research on *African American families* has primarily focused on _____ and _____ families.

10. *Functionalists* are not only interested in intended, overt, or _____ *functions* of social institutions, but also the unintended, unrecognized, or _____ *functions* as well.

11. *Talcott Parsons*, a structural-functionalist, emphasized that a differentiation of gender roles within a family is a functional necessity for the solidarity of the marriage relationship. He described the male role as _____ and the female role as _____.

12. *Karl Marx* believed that two classes with fundamentally opposing interests as well as unequal power existed in modern industrial society which he called the _____ (owners) and the _____ (workers).

13. According to proponents of the *conflict perspective*, the source of male dominance and women's subordination is the _____ and _____.

14. The _____ is the process whereby people assign meanings to social phenomena.

15. Using the *symbolic-interactionist perspective,* sociologist *Jessie Bernard* argued that men and women are likely to view and experience marriage _____.

16. _____ *theory* assumes humans are rational, calculating beings who consciously weigh the costs versus the benefits of their relationships.

17. Although *life cycle theories* give us important insights into the complexities of family life, a shortcoming is that they assume that most families are _____ families with _____.

18. *Liberal feminists theory* assumes that at the basis of women's inequality is _____.

19. In general, the _____ *perspective* begins with the basic premise that there is no hierarchy of oppression. Men, like women, are oppressed by a social conditioning that makes them incapable of developing and expressing a wide range of personality traits or skills and limits their expressions.

20. A major criticism of the new politics of masculinity concerns its view of men as *primary* _____.

Short-Answer

1. Define the concepts of *theory* and *hypothesis*. Develop an hypothesis and define the variables you identify. Which theoretical perspective discussed in the chapter seems to best explain why you think you hypothesis is accurate? Why?

2. What are the five procedures identified in the text that represent the *scientific method*?

3. What are the major *research methods* used by sociologists for the study of marriages and families? Briefly describe each method. What is one relative advantage and disadvantage when studying marriages and families for each of these

4. Briefly describe the scientific methodologies used by *feminist researchers*.

5. Briefly describe the conclusions by Peter Blau and Otis Duncan concerning *social mobility patterns* in the United States. What was a major weakness in their methodology?

6. Scientific research does not exist in a vacuum. Its theory and practice reflect the structure and values of U.S. society. Given this reality, what are the qualities of research that must be evaluated to properly interpret research results and conclusions?

7. The authors of the text focus on several *theoretical perspectives*. Select two of these perspectives and discuss how each orients researchers to the study of marriages and families. Identify basic assumptions, key concepts, and general arguments being used by proponents of each perspective you select.

8. Differentiate between *qualitative* and *quantitative* research. What are the relative advantages and disadvantages of each method?

9. What do the authors mean when they talk about the need for a *new scholarship* on marriages and families?

PART VI: ANSWERS TO STUDY QUESTIONS

True-False

1.	T	(p. 30)	11.	T	(p. 40)
2.	T	(p. 31)	12.	T	(p. 42)
3.	T	(p. 31)	13.	F	(p. 43)
4.	T	(p. 32)	14.	T	(p. 44)
5.	T	(p. 33)	15.	F	(p. 46)
6.	F	(p. 33)	16.	F	(p. 46)
7.	F	(p. 36)	17.	T	(p. 46)
8.	F	(p. 36)	18.	T	(p. 48)
9.	T	(p. 46)	19.	F	(p. 50)
10.	F	(p. 39)	20.	T	(p. 52)

Multiple-Choice

1.	c	(p. 31)	12.	d	(p. 38)
2.	d	(p. 31)	13.	a	(p. 38)
3.	c	(p. 31)	14.	b	(p. 40)
4.	a	(p. 31)	15.	c	(p. 42)
5.	e	(p. 33)	16.	c	(p. 43)
6.	c	(p. 33)	17.	d	(p. 44)
7.	c	(p. 35)	18.	e	(p. 45)
8.	b	(p. 35)	19.	d	(p. 46)
9.	b	(p. 35)	20.	e	(p. 47)
10.	a	(p. 36)	21.	a	(p. 49)
11.	e	(p. 36)	22.	d	(p. 50)

Matching

1.	l	(pp. 45-46)
2.	f	(p. 42)
3.	o	(p. 44)
4.	h	(p. 31)
5.	j	(p. 40)
6.	c	(p. 43)
7.	g	(p. 47)
8.	e	(p. 31)

9.	i	(p. 35)
10.	p	(p. 46)
11.	k	(p. 49)
12.	a	(p. 43)
13.	n	(p. 47)
14.	b	(p. 33)
15.	m	(pp. 35-36)
16.	d	(p. 33)

Fill-In

1. theory (p. 31)
2. empirical (p. 31)
3. scientific method (p. 31)
4. Reliability (p. 33)
5. questionnaires, interviews (p. 33)
6. ethnography. (pp. 35-36)
7. Quantitative, Qualitative (p. 36)
8. education, social origins (p. 38)
9. lower, working-class (p. 40)
10. manifest, latent (p. 42)
11. instrumental, affective (p 42)
12. capitalists, proletariat (p. 44)
13. home, family (p. 45)
14. social construction of reality (p. 46)
15. differently (p. 46)
16. Social exchange (p. 47)
17. nuclear, children, (p. 49)
18. sexism (p. 50)
19. men's studies (p. 52)
20. victims (p. 53)

PART VII: IN FOCUS—MAJOR ISSUES

- The Sociology of Marriages and Families

  How is the sociological view of marriages and families different than our everyday, personal views of these social institutions?

- Studying Marriages and Families: The Link Between Research and Theory

  What is a theory?

  What is the scientific method?

What are the steps in the *scientific research process*?

- Methodological Techniques in the Study of Marriages and Families

  Briefly define each of the following:

  surveys

  observation

  case studies

  ethnography

- A Critical Look at Traditional Research on Marriages and Families

  What do our authors point out about the history of research on marriages and families in terms of which groups have been underrepresented or misrepresented?

- Theoretical Perspectives

  Briefly summarize the follows perspectives on marriage and families. Identify key terms and the main ideas for each perspective.

  structural functionalism

  conflict theory

29

symbolic interactionism

social-exchange theory

social constructionism

the developmental family life cycle model

feminist theory

- Men's Studies Relative to Marriages and Families

  What is meant by the new politics of masculinity? What are your reactions?

PART VIII: ANALYSIS AND COMMENT

- Searching the Internet: Characteristics of the Welfare Population (p. 34)

  Key Points: Comments/Questions:

- In Other Places: Marriage and Family Patterns in Kenya (p. 41)

  Key Points: Comments/Questions:

- **Applying the Sociological Imagination: Developing a Minitheory (p. 53)**

    Key Points: Questions/Comments:

- **Writing Your Own Script: The Family Life Cycle: Locating Your Family (p. 54)**

    Key Points: Questions/Comments:

31

3 Understanding Gender: Its Influence in Intimate Relationships

PART I: CHAPTER OUTLINE

I.   Distinguishing Sex and Gender Roles
    A.   Sex Differences
    B.   The Process of Sex Differentiation
    C.   Gender Differences: The Nature-Nurture Debate
II.   Traditional Meanings of Femininity and Masculinity
    A.   Traditional Gender Roles: Female and Male
    B.   Gender Variations: Race, Class, and Culture
III.   Gender Roles in Transition
IV.   Theories of Gender Role Socialization
    A.   Psychoanalytic/Identification Theory
    B.   Social-Learning Theory
    C.   Cognitive-Development Theory
    D.   Enculturated-Lens Theory
V.   Agents of Socialization
    A.   Parents
    B.   Teachers
    C.   The Mass Media
VI.   Consequences of Gender Stereotyping
    A.   Lifestyle Choices
    B.   Self-Esteem
    C.   Self-Confidence
    D.   Mental Health
    E.   Women, Men, and Friends
    F.   Patterns of Communication
VII.   Changing Realities, Changing Roles
VIII.   Summary
IX.   Key Terms
X.   Questions for Study and Reflection
XI.   Further Reading

PART II: LEARNING OBJECTIVES

1.   To be able to distinguish between the concepts of sex and gender.
2.   To begin to see the connection between ascribed and achieved statuses and role expectations for females and males.
3.   To become aware of the components of thee nature-nurture debate concerning gender differences.

4. To evaluate the effects of gender stereotyping.
5. To describe traditional gender roles and traditional meanings of femininity and masculinity.
6. To begin to consider ways in which gender roles are changing in our society.
7. To review and evaluate four theories of gender-role socialization.
8. To identify and the agents of socialization and describe how they provide gender-role socialization.

PART III: KEY TERMS

agents of socialization

androgynous

achieved status

ascribed status

berdache

cognitive-development theory

content analysis

enculturated-lens theory

gender

gender role socialization

gender role stereotype

gender identity

hermaphoditism

intersexuality

master status

modeling

Oedipus complex

psychoanalytic/identification theory

role

self-esteem

sex

social-learning theory

status

transsexuals

PART IV: IMPORTANT RESEARCHERS

Sandra Bem   Nancy Chodorow

Erik Erikson   Sigmund Freud

Karen Horney   Lawrence Kohlbeg

Janet Lever   Maria Lepowski

John Money and Anke Ehrhardt   Deborah Tannen

PART V: STUDY QUESTIONS

True-Fale

1. Rigid role definitions lead to the development of *gender role stereotypes*. T F
2. *Gender* is a concept referring to the physiological characteristics that differentiate between females and males. T F
3. One pair of a human's 46 chromosomes, the sex chromosomes, determines whether a fertilized egg will develop into a female (XX) or male (XY) fetus. T F
4. Cross-cultural research on gender roles reveals little if any consistency in traits typically defined as *masculine* or *feminine*. T F
5. *Margaret Mead's* anthropological research in New Guinea revealed tremendous cross-cultural similarity in gender role patterns. T F
6. Surveys reveal that most women and men in the United States agree that it would be better if women could stay home and just take care of the house and children. T F
7. According to *Sigmund Freud's psychoanalytic theory*, it is during the phallic stage of personality development that boys and girls proceed in different direction. T F

8. *Social-learning theory* (behaviorism) focuses on the significant impact of biology, especially genes, on gender behavior. T F

9. According to *cognitive-development theory*, a child's mind matures through interaction with the surrounding environment, with the child taking an active role in her or his world. T F

10. *Enculturated-lens theory* focuses on how anatomical and physiological differences between females and males determine gender role patterns. T F

11. *Janet Lever's* research on gender suggests that girls' activities have *more complicated rules* than boys' activities. T F

12. Children's television shows tend to have more male than female characters. T F

13. *Self-esteem* refers to the overall feelings—positive or negative—that a person has about herself or himself. T F

14. Men have higher rates of *depression* than women. T F

15. Men's *friendships*, in contrast to women's, tend to focus more on shared activities. T F

Multiple-Choice

1. In 1999 a jury awarded Kevin Knussman $375,000 because:

    (a) he had requested, and was denied, extended leave from his job to care for his newborn daughter.
    (b) he had serious complications resulting from elective surgery.
    (c) he was denied custody rights because of the type of job he held.
    (d) he had sued his wife for earnings he felt he deserved for household labor performed over a twenty year marriage.

2. Sociologists use the term _____ to refer to a set of expected behaviors associated with a specific position, or _____.

    (a) status, role
    (b) status, model
    (c) role, status
    (d) model, role

3. Which of the following would be an example of an *ascribed status*?

    (a) teacher
    (b) parent
    (c) student
    (d) spouse
    (e) male

4.   _____ refers to the socially learned behavior associated with being either male or female.

   (a)   Sex
   (b)   Status
   (c)   Gender
   (d)   Gender identity
   (e)   Sexual orientation

5.   Occasionally a developing fetus is exposed to feminizing and masculizing hormones at inappropriate times. Scientists refer to the individual who is born as:

   (a)   transsexual.
   (b)   androgynous.
   (c)   asexual.
   (d)   intersexed.

6.   Anthropologists have described a *third gender*, found in several other cultures, known as:

   (a)   hermaphrodites.
   (b)   androgens.
   (c)   berdache.
   (d)   ahila.
   (e)   baganza.

7.   Research on undergraduates in the U.S. found that the male stereotype was more _____ defined than that of the female.

   (a)   negatively
   (b)   rigidly
   (c)   broadly
   (d)   meaningfully

8.   Among the Vanatinai people who live on an island of the coast of Papua New Guinea, anthropologist Maria Lepowsky found:

   (a)   a third gender.
   (b)   gender equality.
   (c)   a gender hierarchy in which feminine traits are seen as superior to masculine traits.
   (d)   evidence among a primitive stone age people to support Freud's psychoanalytic theory.

9.   Who among the following believed that children learn gender appropriate behavior by unconsciously identifying with the same-sex parent as they pass through the *phallic stage* of development?

   (a)   Jean Piaget
   (b)   Charles Horton Cooley
   (c)   Lawrence Kohlberg
   (d)   Sigmund Freud
   (e)   Karen Horney

10. Which of the following theories of gender-role socialization would be most likely to use the term *modeling*?

   (a) identification
   (b) cognitive development
   (c) enculturated-lens
   (d) social-learning
   (e) Freudian

11. This researcher understands gender as emerging from the social organization of parenting roles. Implicit in this researcher's view is the belief that shared parenting between women and men would be beneficial to society.

   (a) Nancy Chodorow
   (b) Sigmund Freud
   (c) Erik Erikson
   (d) Charales Horton Cooley

12. According to *Lawrence Kohlberg's* adaptation of *cognitive-development theory*:

   (a) about age 2-3 children become aware that two sexes exist.
   (b) gender identity does not develop until children are 6-7 years old and have the mental ability to grasp the concept of constancy or permanency.
   (c) once gender identity is developed, children are able to organize their behavior around it.
   (d) the emergence of children's gender identity can be explained.
   (e) all of the above.

13. According to *Sandra Bem's enculturated-lens theory*, what gender issues need to be focused upon?

   (a) gender polarization
   (b) androcentrism
   (c) biological essentialism
   (d) all of the above

14. According to *Janet Lever,* why do boys' games provide more training for leadership than girls' games?

   (a) They are based on competition.
   (b) They have complex rules.
   (c) Boys' play groups are larger.
   (d) All of the above.

15. *Content analysis* of children's television shows reveals:

    (a) they feature more than twice as many male as female roles.
    (b) females are more likely to be found in minor roles with little responsibility for the outcome of the story and are rarely shown working outside the home.
    (c) male characters are depicted in a variety of occupations to which many boys realistically can aspire.
    (d) children, especially girls, are aware of the narrowness of television's portrayal of girl's lives.
    (e) all of the above.

16. Concerning *prime-time television programming* which of the following has research found as patterns?

    (a) Besides being younger, female characters are typically thin, physically attractive, and scantily attired.
    (b) The overwhelmingly majority of commercials advertising products to enhance personal appearance are aimed at girls.
    (c) The vast majority of programs depict women in a limited range of roles.
    (d) All of the above.

17. Rigid adherence to *traditional gender-role norms* may interfere with the development of good mental health for:

    (a) men.
    (b) women.
    (c) both men and women.
    (d) actually, such gender-role norms are shown to be healthy for both men and women.

18. According to *Deborah Tannen*, women and men speak different languages. Women speak and hear a language of intimacy and connectedness. Men on the other hand speak and hear a language of:

    (a) order and rapport.
    (b) status and independence.
    (c) negotiation and exploitation.
    (d) conflict and strength.

19. According to *Deborah Tannen*, women are more likely to use a _____ *talk style* of conversation.

    (a) rapport
    (b) response
    (c) report
    (d) reflective

20.   *Sandra Bem* suggests that in order to reach greater gender equality:

    (a)   parents need to teach children that the only definitive gender differences are anatomical and reproductive.
    (b)   Parents need to help children substitute an "individual differences" schema for the "gender" schema that currently exists.
    (c)   both (a) and (b).
    (d)   none of the above.

Matching

a.	ascribed statuses	h.	ethnomethodology
b.	sex	i.	social-learning theory
c.	cognitive development theory	j.	gender
d.	psychoanalytic/identification theory	k.	a genetic male
e.	berdache	l.	a genetic female
f.	transsexuals	m.	enculturated-lens
g.	gender identity	n.	gender role stereotypes

1.   Male, female, daughter, son, African American, white. _____
2.   A person's awareness of being female or male. _____
3.   A theory suggesting that children learn gender-appropriate behaviors by unconsciously identifying with their some-sex parent and that they pass through a series of stages in their development. _____
4.   Asserts that gender roles and gender identity are learned directly through a system of positive reinforcement (rewards) and negative reinforcement (punishments) and indirectly from observation and modeling. _____
5.   Fundamental to this theory is the belief that the child's mind matures through interaction with the surrounding environment. _____
6.   Socially learned behaviors, attitudes, and expectations that are associated with being female or male. _____
7.   The biological aspects of a person—the physiological characteristics that differentiate females from males. _____
8.   Oversimplified expectations of what it means to be a woman or a man. _____
9.   Persons who believe they were born with the body of the wrong sex. _____
10.   Individuals found in many Native American cultures who adopted the gender associated to members of the opposite sex. _____
11.   Chromosomally XY. _____
12.   A theory arguing that gender role acquisition is greatly influenced by hidden cultural assumptions about how societal members should look, behave, and feel, and that are so deeply embedded in social institutions that they are systematically reproduced from one generation to the next. _____

Fill-In

1.   Sociologists use the term _____ to refer to a set of expected behaviors associated with a specific status.
2.   Positions we are born into and others which we have little control over are referred to as _____ *statuses.*
3.   _____ refers to a person's awareness of being female or male.

4. Our biological sex is established at the moment of conception. The father's genetic contribution determines the child's sex, in that he provides either an _____ or a _____ *chromosome*, whereas the mother always provides an _____ chromosome.

5. People who believe they were born with the body of the wrong sex are called _____.

6. A research methodology that allows respondents to rate the degree to which traits characterize both the typical man and the typical woman found several interesting patterns. One pattern was that two sets of *adjectives* become evident. The *prototypical woman* was described as _____ and _____, and the *prototypical man* was described as _____ and _____.

7. _____ *theory* maintains that behavior that is regularly followed by a reward is more likely to be repeated.

8. *Lawrence Kohlberg* adopted _____ *theory* to explain the emergence of children's gender identities. Fundamental to this theory is the belief that the child's mind matures through interaction with the surrounding environment.

9. *Sandra Bem*, using *enculturated-lens theory* focuses on three issues, including gender _____, _____, and _____ essentialism.

10. Parents, the mass media, peers, and teachers, in the text as _____.

11. *Janet Lever* found many differences between girls and boys *activities*. She believes boys activities better prepare them to succeed in modern industrial society as compared to girls because the rules for these activities are _____.

12. The averaged school-aged child in the United States watches approximately _____ *hours* of television every week.

13. Eighty-six percent of *commercials* advertising products to enhance personal appearance are aimed at _____.

14. The authors suggest that at least two factors seem to play a crucial role in the relationship between *gender* and *self-esteem:* _____ and _____.

15. According to research cited in the text, _____ is a central part of *women's friendships. Men's friendships,* in contrast, focus more on shared _____.

16. According to *Deborah Tannen*, women speak and hear a *language of* _____ and _____, whereas men speak and hear a *language of* _____ and _____.

17. Psychologist *Sandra Bem* suggests that parents tell children that the only definitive gender differences are _____ and _____, and that they use the "individual differences" schema rather than "gender differences" schema for organizing and processing information.

Short-Answer

1. Differentiate between the terms *sex* and *gender.*

2. What examples from your own life can be used to illustrate *gender stereotyping*?

3. What does the information in *Figure 3-1* (p. 58) suggest about the nature-nurture debate?

4. What patterns have been found cross-culturally on traditional meanings of *femininity* and *masculinity*?

5. What is the cross-cultural evidence concerning the universality of certain *gender role traits*?

6. What is the evidence being provided by the authors that suggests gender roles in our society are in *transition*?

7. Four theories of *gender role socialization* are reviewed in the text. Which of these most appeals to you personally as a way of explaining gender role patterns in our society? Why?

8. What are the major *agents of socialization* as reviewed in the text? Using you own experiences to illustrate, discuss how each agent has influenced your gender identity.

9. Four *consequences of gender stereotyping* are discussed in the text. What are these? What is the evidence provided by the authors for each of the four? What are you opinions on this issue?

10. Women and men seem to have different kinds of relationships with *friends*. What are the findings on this subject as reported in the text? Do you agree, based on personal experience, with these findings and interpretations? Why?

PART VI: ANSWERS TO STUDY QUESTIONS

True-False

1.	T	(p. 57)	9.	T	(p. 66)
2.	F	(p. 57)	10.	F	(p. 67)
3.	T	(p. 58)	11.	F	(p. 69)
4.	F	(p. 61)	12.	T	(p. 71)
5.	F	(p. 62)	13.	T	(p. 74)
6.	T	(p. 63)	14.	F	(p. 76)
7.	T	(p. 65)	15.	T	(p. 77)
8.	F	(p. 65)			

Multiple-Choice

1.	a	(p. 56)	11.	a	(p. 65)
2.	c	(p. 57)	12.	e	(p. 66)
3.	e	(p. 57)	13.	d	(p. 67)
4.	c	(p. 57)	14.	d	(p. 69)
5.	d	(p. 59)	15.	e	(p. 71)
6.	c	(p. 60)	16.	d	(p. 71-72)
7.	b	(p. 62)	17.	c	(p. 76)
8.	b	(p. 62)	18.	b	(p. 78)
9.	d	(p. 64)	19.	a	(p. 78)
10.	d	(p. 65)	20.	c	(p. 79)

Matching

1.	a	(p. 57)	7.	b	(p. 57)
2.	g	(p. 58)	8.	n	(p. 57)
3.	d	(p. 64)	9.	f	(p. 59)
4.	I	(p. 65)	10.	e	(p. 60)
5.	c	(p. 66)	11.	k	(p. 58)
6.	j	(p. 57)	12.	m	(p. 67)

<u>Fill-In</u>

1. role (p. 57)
2. ascribed (p. 58)
3. Gender identity (p. 58)
4. X, Y, X (p. 58)
5. transsexuals (p. 59)
6. nice, nurturant, potent, powerful (p. 61)
7. social-learning (p. 65)
8. cognitive-development (p. 66)
9. polarization, androcentrism, biological (p. 67)
10. agents of socialization (p. 67)
11. more complex (p. 69)
12. 27 (p. 70
13. girls (p. 72)
14. age, sex typing (p. 74)
15. conversation, activities (p. 77)
16. intimacy, connectedness, status, independence (p. 78)
17. anatomical, reproductive (p. 79)

PART VII: IN FOCUS—IMPORTANT ISSUES

- Distinguishing Sex and Gender Roles

    What is the evidence being presented in the text concerning gender differences and the *nature-nurture debate*?

- Traditional Meanings of Femininity and Masculinity

    What are the traditional understandings of gender and gender roles for women and men?

    What is the relationship between gender, race, and class in our society?

- Gender Roles in Transition

    What is the evidence that gender roles are in transition in our society?

42

- Theories of Gender Role Socialization

    Describe how each of the following theories explains the socialization process with respect to the acquisition of gender role:

    Psychoanalytic/Identification

    Social-Learning

    Cognitive-Development

    Enculturated-Lens

- Agents of Socialization

    Provide an illustration for each of the following as an agent of gender role socialization:

    Parents—clothing, toys and games, chores, language, peers and play activities

    Teachers

    The mass media—children's shows, prime-time television

- Consequences of Gender Stereotyping

  What is gender stereotyping related to each of the following?

  Lifestyle choices:

  Self-esteem:

  Self-confidence:

  Mental health:

  Friendships:

  Patterns of communication:

- Changing Realities, Changing Roles

  What are your expectations about how gender roles will change in our society over the next century?

PART VIII: ANALYSIS AND COMMENT

- In Other Place: "Gender Equality in Vanatinai…and Backlash in Bangladesh" (p. 62)

  Key Points: Questions/Comments

- Strengthening Marriages and Families: "Resolving Gender Issues" (p. 64)

  Key Points: Questions/Comments:

- Social Policy Issues: "Boys and Men are Gendered, Too" (p. 75)

    Key Points: Questions/Comments:

- Applying the Sociological Imagination: "Gendered Communication" (p. 79)

    Key Points: Questions/Comments:

- Writing Your Own Script: "Reflections on Gender" (p. 80)

    Key Points: Questions/Comments:

4 The Many Faces Of Love

PART II: LEARNING OBJECTIVES

1.   To recognize the complex nature of the concept love.
2.   To understand the concept of romantic love from a historical perspective.
3.   To be able to identify and describe the different ways in which people express love.
4.   To be able to differentiate between love, friendship, infatuation, and liking.
5.   To gain insight into the nature of love through the application of three explanations of love today--the wheel theory, limerance theory, and the social-exchange theory.
6.   To be able to describe the gender differences in love relationships, compare lesbian and gay love relationships, and heterosexual relationships among African Americans.
7.   To identify and understand some of the obstacles to love and loving relationships, including traditional gender role socialization, patriarchy, lack of trust, jealousy, and envy.
8.   To consider how romantic love will be influenced by social forces during the twenty-first century.

PART III: KEY TERMS

androgynous

courtly love

envy

feminization of love

infatuation

jealousy

liking

love map

romantic love

wheel theory of love

trust

PART IV: IMPORTANT RESEARCHERS

Erich Fromm   Morton Hunt

Robert Karen   Ralph Hupka

John Allen Lee   Plato

Ira Reiss   John Rempel and John Holmes

Zick Rubin   Robert Sternberg

Lynn Smith and Gordon Clayton Dorothy Tennov

PART V: STUDY QUESTIONS

True-False

1. A major difference between *romantic love* and other types of love is the element of *eroticism*.   T   F
2. *Homosexuality* was viewed with disgust in ancient Greek society.   T   F
3. The notion of *courtly love* had little influence on Western thought on romantic behavior.   T   F
4. In contrast to traditional Chinese culture, romantic love and sexuality are far less important than other factors as a basis for intimate relation.   T   F
5. The concept *storge* depicts a style of loving that is unexciting and uneventful.   T   F
6. Research has demonstrated that women and men show gender differences in *styles of loving*, however not significantly in terms or eros and agape.   T   F
7. Research suggests that *friendship* is more unstable than romantic love.   T   F
8. *Infatuation* refers to a strong attraction to another person based on an idealized picture of that other person.   T   F
9. According to *Ira Reiss' wheel theory of love*, most people fall in love at first sight.   T   F
10. *Ira Reiss* suggests in his *wheel theory of love* that a key factor in the interpersonal processes of rapport is social background.   T   F
11. *Limerance theory* uses economic principles in explaining why people fall in love.   T   F
12. Research has found that females distinguish much more sharply between *liking* and *loving* than males do.   T   F
13. Research has found that men *fall in love* sooner and harder than women.   T   F
14. An *androgynous* view of sex validates both feminine and masculine styles of loving.   T   F

15. A major difference between gay/lesbian relationships and heterosexual relationships seems to be in the manner in which the love relationships develop and in their duration.   T   F
16. *Envy* refer to unhappiness or discontent with ourselves that arises from the belief that something about ourselves does not measure up to someone else's level.   T   F
17. Research indicates that men feel *jealousy* more intensely than women do, and that it causes men more suffering and distress.   T   F

Multiple-Choice

1. Although a common thread of caring is woven trough all love relationships, the major difference between these feelings of love and *romantic love* is the element of:

   (a) agape.
   (b) storge.
   (c) eroticism.
   (d) friendship.
   (e) commitment.

2. A _____ refers to a group of physical, psychological, and behavioral traits that one finds attractive.

   (a) love map
   (b) master status
   (c) quality complex
   (d) love set

3. Which of the following is *not* a type of love as identified by *Plato*?

   (a) eros
   (b) agape
   (c) philos
   (d) thanatos

4. According to the text, what led to the belief that love should occur before, not after marriage?

   (a) industrialization
   (b) ideals of ancient Rome
   (c) ideals of ancient Greece
   (d) early Christian notions

5. According to *Erich Fromm*, the essential *components of love* are:

   (a) care, responsibility, respect, and knowledge.
   (b) sex, identity, and security.
   (c) passion, intimacy, and attachment.
   (d) companionship, friendship, concern, and faith.

6. Who defined love in terms of a *triangle-like* relationship among three components:

   (a)   Erich Fromm
   (b)   Plato
   (c)   Jessie Bernard
   (d)   Ernie Davie
   (e)   Robert Sternberg

7. According to *John Allen Lee, manic love* is characterized by obsession and is a combination of:

   (a)   eros and storge.
   (b)   ludus and storge.
   (c)   friendship and infatuation.
   (d)   eros and ludus.
   (e)   pragma and agape.

8. According to *Keith Davis* and *Michael Todd* spontaneity, enjoyment, and trust are all characteristics of:

   (a)   love.
   (b)   liking.
   (c)   friendship.
   (d)   infatuation.

9. Which of the following is *not* true of *infatuation*?

   (a)   it has a strong sexual element
   (b)   it focuses on a specific characteristic of the person
   (c)   it is long lasting
   (d)   it is superficial

10. *Ira Reiss'* _____ theory of love proposes that love involves four major interpersonal processes: rapport, self-revelation, mutual dependence, and need fulfillment.

    (a)   color
    (b)   wheel
    (c)   ladder
    (d)   limerance
    (e)   quadrangle

11. *Dorothy Tennov* uses the term _____ to refer to a style of love characterized by an extreme attraction, a complete absorption or obsessive preoccupation of one person with another.

    (a)   agape
    (b)   rapport
    (c)   mania
    (d)   eros
    (e)   limerance

12. In studying the difference between *liking* and *loving*, *Zick Rubin* found that:

    (a) females distinguish much more sharply between liking and loving than males do.
    (b) men tend to start a relationship with a much more romantic perspective than females.
    (c) men tend to fall in love more quickly and earlier than females.
    (d) men are more likely than women to have crushes and to fall in love with someone who doesn't love them in return.
    (e) all of the above.

13. Researcher *Francesca Cancian* described the gender differences in love relationships in terms of:

    (a) an emasculation of males.
    (b) a romanticizing of sex.
    (c) the dominance of women.
    (d) the feminization of love.

14. Research on *lesbian* and *gay* love relationships has found:

    (a) a difference in how love relationships develop compared to heterosexual love relationships.
    (b) the duration of the relationships compared to heterosexual love relationships.
    (c) the stability of the relationships compared to heterosexual love relationships.
    (d) that lesbian love relationships tend to be more stable than gay love relationships.
    (e) all of the above.

15. According to *Robert Karen*:

    (a) men get much more out of love relationships than they give.
    (b) women get much more out of love relationships than they give.
    (c) men and women share equally in love relationships.
    (d) gay and lesbian couples experience love differently than heterosexual couples.
    (e) patriarchy inhibits the development of love in marriage.

16. *John Rupel* and *John Holmes* identified three basic elements of _____: *predictability, dependability,* and *faith*.

    (a) love
    (b) trust
    (c) jealousy
    (d) limerance
    (e) envy

17. The thoughts and feelings that emerge when an actual or desired relationship is believed to be threatened refers to:

    (a)   envy.
    (b)   limerance.
    (c)   jealousy.
    (d)   trust.

18. Cross-cultural research on *jealousy* reveals:

    (a)   it is not biologically determined; rather it is a learned emotion.
    (b)   its existence and expression depend very much on how love and love relationships are defined.
    (c)   is rooted in the social structure of a society insofar as cultural norms provide the cues that will or will not trigger.
    (d)   all of the above.

Matching

a.	trust	k.	philos
b.	agape	l.	wheel theory
c.	Erich Fromm	m.	friendship
d.	infatuation	n.	love
e.	limerance	o.	envy
f.	androgyny	p.	consumate love
g.	love map	q.	Plato
h.	derived	r.	secondary
i.	primary	s.	jealousy
j.	romantic love	t.	liking

1. The intense feelings, emotions, and thoughts coupled with sexual passion and erotic expression that a person directs toward another as well as the ideology, the set of beliefs, that upholds it. ____
2. Includes the components of commitment, passion, and intimacy. ____
3. Defined love as the highest expression of human virtue because of its ability to inspire people to be kind, honorable, and wise. ____
4. According to William Good, a strong emotional attachment, a cathexis, between adolescents or adults of opposite sexes, with at least the components of sex, desire, and tenderness. ___
5. A selfless love, it is spontaneous and altruistic and requires nothing in return. ____
6. Identified four essential components of love--care, responsibility, respect, and knowledge. ____
7. According to John Alan Lee, eros, ludus, and storge are examples of this style of love. ____
8. Involves a strong attraction to another person based on an idealized picture of that person. ____
9. A theory of love proposing that love involves four major interpersonal processes--rapport, self-revelation, mutual dependence, and need fulfillment. ____
10. A style of love characterized by an extreme attraction, a complete absorption, or obsessive preoccupation of one person with another. ____
11. The thoughts and feelings that emerge when an actual or desired relationship is believed to be threatened. ____

12. The degree of confidence a person feels when she or he thinks about a relationship. ____
13. Qualities include--enjoyment, mutual assistance, spontaneity, acceptance, respect, trust, understanding, and confidence--but not passion. ____
14. Unhappiness or discontent with ourselves that arises from the belief something about ourselves does not measure up to someone else's level. ____
15. A group of physical, psychological, and behavioral traits that one finds attractive. ____

Fill-In

1. Although a common thread of caring is woven through all love relationships, the major difference between these feelings of love and *romantic love* is the element of _____.
2. According to a _____ point of view, love can only be understood as symbolic or a social construction that by itself has no intrinsic meaning.
3. Most writers trace contemporary notions of *romantic love* to _____ society.
4. _____ *love* combined two basic ideas of the time period (1000-1300 A.D.) male chivalry and the idealization of women.
5. The main difference between love in *ancient Roman society* and *courtly love* is that the latter was basically _____.
6. Among the *!Kung* of southern Africa, love is an important commodity for women, and it is intimately connected to their sexuality. In *traditional* _____ *culture*, romantic love and sexuality are far less important.
7. According to *Erich Fromm*, the four essential *components of love* include _____, _____, _____, and _____.
8. According to *John Allen Lee's* analysis, the *derived styles* of love include _____, _____, and _____.
9. _____ involves a strong attachment to another person based on an idealized picture of that person.
10. *Zick Rubin* found that *females* distinguish much more sharply between _____ and _____ than males do.
11. The four major interpersonal processes in *Ira Reiss' wheel theory* include _____, _____, _____, and _____.
12. Because of societal disapproval, *gay lovers* frequently look to each other to satisfy all their needs, Thus *gay love* is often more _____ and sometimes _____.
13. A major difference between heterosexual and gay or lesbian couples seems to be in the manner in which the *love relationship* _____ and in its _____.
14. Some evidence suggests that there is a difference in the way African Americans and whites view love. Some research indicates that *African Americans* tend to have a more _____ view of love.
15. According to researchers *John Rempel* and *John Holmes*, the three elements of *trust* include _____, _____, and _____.
16. _____ refers to the thoughts and feelings that emerge when an actual or desired relationship is believed to be threatened.

Short-Answer

1. Briefly recount the historical development of *romantic love* in Western society.
2. Differentiate between how love was understood in *ancient Greek* and *ancient Roman* societies.
3. What was *courtly love*? What is its connection to our modern understanding of romantic love?
4. How did *industrialization* affect the development of love in Western societies?

5. Differentiate between *Erich Fromm's* and *Robert Sternberg's* perspectives on love.
6. Provide illustrations of the *primary* and *derived* styles of love using *John Alan Lee's color wheel theory*.
7. Differentiate between *friendship, infatuation,* and *liking*.
8. Identify the major differences between love relationships as experienced and understood by *females* and *males*.
9. What generalizations are being made concerning differences and similarities between *gay and lesbian* and *heterosexual* love relationships?
10. What generalizations are being made concerning differences and similarities between love relationship among *African American* and *whites*?
11. How is *jealousy* experienced differently by women and men?
12. What points are the authors making about *love* in the twenty-first century?

PART VI: ANSWERS TO STUDY QUESTIONS

True-False

1.	T	(p. 83)	10.	T	(p. 95-96)
2.	F	(p. 85)	11.	F	(p. 97)
3.	F	(p. 86)	12.	T	(p. 98)
4.	T	(p. 88)	13.	T	(p. 99)
5.	T	(p. 91)	14.	T	(p. 100)
6.	T	(p. 92)	15.	T	(p. 100)
7.	F	(p. 93)	16.	T	(p. 105)
8.	T	(p. 94)	17.	F	(p. 107)
9.	F	(p. 95)			

Multiple-Choice

1.	c	(p. 83)	10.	b	(p. 95)
2.	a	(p. 84)	11.	e	(p. 97)
3.	d	(p. 85)	12.	e	(p. 98-99)
4.	a	(p. 87)	13.	d	(p. 99)
5.	a	(p. 90)	14.	e	(p. 100-101)
6.	e	(p. 90)	15.	a	(p. 103)
7.	d	(p. 91)	16.	b	(p. 104)
8.	c	(p. 93)	17.	c	(p. 105)
9.	c	(p. 94)	18.	d	(p. 106)

Matching

1.	j	(p. 83)	9.	l	(p. 95)
2.	p	(p. 90)	10.	e	(p. 97)
3.	q	(p. 85)	11.	s	(p. 105)
4.	n	(p. 83)	12.	a	(p. 104)
5.	b	(p. 85)	13.	m	(p. 93)
6.	c	(p. 90)	14.	o	(p. 105)
7.	i	(p. 91)	15.	g	(p. 84)
8.	d	(p. 94)			

1.   eroticism (p. 83)
2.   social constructionist (p. 84)
3.   Greek (p. 85)
4.   Courtly (p. 86)
5.   nonsexual (p. 86)
6.   Chinese (p. 88)
7.   care, responsibility, respect, knowledge (p. 90)
8.   mania, pragma, agape (pp. 91-92)
9.   Infatuation (p. 94)
10.   liking, loving (p. 95)
11.   rapport, self-revelation, mutual dependence, fulfillment of personality needs (pp. 95-96)
12.   intense, possessive (p. 100)
13.   develops, duration (p. 100)
14.   romantic (p. 102)
15.   predictability, confidence, faith (p. 104)
16.   Jealousy (p. 105)

PART VII: IN FOCUS--IMPORTANT ISSUES

- What Is This Thing Called Love?

  What do our authors mean by saying *love is a social construction*?

  Describe how *love* was generally understood for each of the following periods:

  ancient Greek society

  ancient Roman society

  early Christian idea of love

  Industrial Revolution

- How Do People Express Love?

  Define/describe each of the following types of love as presented in Robert Sternberg's *love triangle:*

  nonlove   empty love

  liking   infatuated love

  companionate love   fatuous love

  romantic love   consumate love

  Define each of the following *primary styles of love:*

  eros

  ludus

  storge

  Define each of the following *derived styles of love*:

  mania

  pragma

  agape

- Love Versus Friendship, Infatuation, and Liking

  What are the characteristics of *friendship* according to researchers Keith Davis and Michael Todd?

  Who is *infatuation* different from love?

  How is *liking* different than love?

- Some Theories of Love

  Describe each of the interpersonal processes in Ira Reiss' *wheel theory of love*:

  Describe love as *limerance*:

  Describe love as *social exchange*:

- Love Across Gender, Sexuality, and Race

  What are four important ways in which women and men tend to differ in terms of love?

  What are three important ways in which lesbian and gay love relationships are different than heterosexual love relationships?

  What are three important points the authors make about female-male African American love relationships?

- Obstacles to Love and Loving Relationships

  How do women and men experience *jealousy* differently?

- Romantic Love in the Twenty-First Century

  What factors are likely to influence romantic love over this next century?

PART VIII: ANALYSIS AND COMMENT

- In Other Places: "The Meaning of Love Across Cultures" (p. 88)

  Key Points: Questions/Comments:

- Applying the Sociological Imagination: "How Does the Media Portray Love?" (p. 100)

  Key Points: Questions/Comments:

- Family Profile: "Pamela Outlar and Betty Crum" (p. 101)

  Key Points: Questions/Comments:

- Writing Your Own Script: "A Social Construction of Love" (p. 108)

  Key Points: Questions/Comments:

5 Dating, Coupling, and Mate Selection

PART I: CHAPTER OUTLINE

I.   Mate Selection In Cross-Cultural and Historical Perspective
      A.   Mate Selection Cross-Culturally
      B.   Mate Selection in the United States: A Historical Perspective
      C.   Functions of Dating: Past and Present

II.   The Intersections of Race, Gender, Class, and Sexual Orientation
      A.   Dating Patterns among African Americans
      B.   The Impact of Gender
      C.   The Impact of Social Class on the Dating Process
      D.   Lesbian and Gay Dating

III.   Theories of Mate Selection
      A.   Exchange Theories
      B.   Filter Theories

IV.   Mate Selection: Finding and Meeting Partners
      A.   The Marriage Market and the Pool of Eligibles
      B.   Freedom versus Constraint in Mate Selection
      C.   Other Factors That Affect Mate Selection
      D.   Personal Qualities and Mate Selection
      E.   The Life Cycle and Mate Selection

V.   Meeting Partners: Where and How
      A.   School, Church, and Work
      B.   Singles' Bars and Gay Bars
      C.   Self-Advertising: Personal Ads
      D.   Dating Clubs and Dating Services
      E.   Video Dating
      F.   Computer Dating
      G.   Dating in Cyberspace

VI.   The Future of Dating

VII.   Violence In Dating and Intimate Relationships
      A.   Physical Abuse
      B.   Date and Acquaintance Rape

VIII. Breaking Up

IX.   Summary

X.   Key Terms

XI.   Questions for Study and Reflection

XII.   Further Reading

PART II: LEARNING OBJECTIVES

1.   To understand mate selection from a historical and cross-cultural perspectives.
2.   To be able to describe the functions of dating, both past and present.
3.   To be able to discuss the impact race, gender, and social class on dating behavior .
4.   To develop an understanding about the dating patterns of lesbians and gays.
5.   To be able to describe and discuss the four theories of mate selection.
6.   To begin to evaluate the influence of physical attraction and companionship on mate selection.
7.   To discuss how people meet potential mates.
8.   To discuss violence and abuse in dating and intimate relationships.

PART III: KEY TERMS

acquaintance rape

anticipatory socialization

arranged marriage

bundling

courtship

cruising

date rape

dating

dowries

endogamy

exogamy

hypergamy

hypogamy

marriage gradient

marriage squeeze

mate selection

pool of eligibles

propinquity

rape

sex ratio

PART IV: IMPORTANT RESEARCHERS

Susan Basow   Allen Bell and Martin Weinberg

Pamela Cytrynbaum   J. N. Edwards

David Klimek   Ersel LeMasters

Bernard Murstein   G. N. Ramu

Phillip Shenon   Susan Steinfirst and Barbara Morgan

PART V: STUDY QUESTIONS

True-False

1. In most traditional (nonindustrialized) societies *mate selection* takes the form of *arranged marriages*. T F
2. Mate selection appears to be a universal feature of human culture—found in all societies around the world. T F
3. Cross-cultural research has found that *arranged marriages* tend to be very stable. T F
4. According to research, given the recent demographic changes in *Chinese* society, the status of women in the mate selection has been declining. T F
5. The *Victorian sex ethic* was not replaced by dating as a means of mate selection in the U.S. until the 1960s. T F

6. During the last decade dating has been based far more on *mutuality* and *sharing* than on traditional gender roles. T F
7. *Dating* has been found by sociologists to be one of the few social phenomena not rotted in social or historical conditions. T F
8. Research by social scientist *Susan Basow* contends that men's dating scripts focus on planning and paying for the date, as well as initiating sexual behavior, whereas women's scripts focus on enhancing their appearance, making conversation, and controlling sexual behavior. T F
9. Dating within the *upper class* of U.S. society tends to be far less regulated than it is for other classes. T F
10. As with heterosexuals, there appear to be some fundamental gender differences in the dating and mate selection behaviors of lesbians and gays. T F
11. Research by *Allen Bell* and *Martin Weinberg* suggests that black gays tend to be more *bisexual* than white gays. T F
12. Two examples of *exchange theories* as identified in the text include *stimulus-value-role theory* and *equity theory*. T F
13. *Exogamy* refers to marriage outside a particular group. T F
14. The *marriage gradient* refers to the demographic condition of there being more men than women in a particular age range within a given population. T F
15. Research has found that we tend to think we are better looking than other people do. Furthermore, men are more likely than women to exaggerate their appearance. T F
16. Most social science literature on dating continues to focus on *college students*, thus in many ways perpetuating the myth that dating is primarily a white, middle-class, college-aged phenomenon. T F
17. Experts project that by the year 2010 less than one-in-four people in the U.S. will be single. T F
18. Although most *rapes* are date or acquaintance rapes, most *reported* rapes are stranger rapes. T F

Multiple-Choice

1. The practice of *dating* is:

    (a)   common in most countries today.
    (b)   not a common practice in most countries today.
    (c)   allowed in most Muslim countries today.
    (d)   a component of courtship that has been around for centuries.

2. Sociologists use the term _____ to refer loosely to the wide range of behavior and social relationships individuals engage in prior to marriage and that lead to long-term or short-term pairings or coupling.

    (a)   dating
    (b)   courtship
    (c)   mate selection
    (d)   anticipatory socialization
    (e)   the marriage gradient

3.   _____ refers to the process of selecting a mate and developing an intimate relationship.

   (a)   Dating
   (b)   Endogamy
   (c)   Mate selection
   (d)   Courtship

4.   In *China* , the ratio of single men to single women over the age of fifteen is:

   (a)   2:1.
   (b)   1:2.
   (c)   6:1.
   (d)   3:1.
   (e)   1:3.

5.   In which of the following cultures has the arranged form of marriage given way to more *free-choice practices*?

   (a)   India
   (b)   Turkey
   (c)   Japan
   (d)   all of the above
   (e)   none of the above

6.   Researchers *Daniel Smith* and *Michael Hindus* have estimated that approximately_____ *percent* of all eighteenth century brides were *pregnant* at the time of their wedding.

   (a)   1
   (b)   20
   (c)   12
   (d)   33
   (e)   60

7.   According to _____, dating patterns of the 1940s involved *six stages* of progressively deepening commitment.

   (a)   Ersel LeMasters
   (b)   Willard Waller
   (c)   Bernard Murstein
   (d)   Reuben Hill
   (e)   Robert Staples

8. Which of the following is *not a function* of dating as summarized by *G.N. Ramu*?

   (a) recreation
   (b) status grading and achievement
   (c) socialization
   (d) mate selection
   (e) attainment of power

9. Socialization that is directed toward learning future roles is known as _____ *socialization*.

   (a) experimental
   (b) anticipatory
   (c) functional
   (d) manifest
   (e) latent

10. The *sex ratio* refers to:

    (a) the pool of eligibles during one's mate selection process.
    (b) the number of men to every 100 women.
    (c) the double standard operating within the mate selection process.
    (d) the erotic dimension of dating and mate selection.

11. Research cited on the text on *gender differences* in courtship behavior revealed:

    (a) women use indirect tactics more often than men.
    (b) men engage in direct verbal contact more often than women.
    (c) when presenting themselves, men stress personal characteristics that are traditionally interpreted as female-valued.
    (d) eye contact is the most frequently used behavior for both women and men.
    (e) all of the above.

12. Which of the following is *not* a conclusion being made by our authors concerning *lesbian* and *gay dating*.

   (a) Like heterosexual couples, most lesbians and gays date for recreational and entertainment purposes, but the development of love relationships is also an important goal.
   (b) Finding a permanent partner is not always easy for lesbians and gays.
   (c) Unlike with heterosexuals, the appears not to be any fundamental gender differences in the dating and mate selection behaviors of lesbians and gays.
   (d) While the subculture of gay bars has been a prime place for gays to meet potential sex partners it has also acted to inhibit long-term partnerships.
   (e) Dating and mating patterns among lesbians and gays do not appear to be significantly different from those found among heterosexual women and men.

13. According to *exchange theory*, who in a relationship has the power?

   (a) the person with the most interest in the relationship
   (b) the person with the least interest in the relationship
   (c) either person, depending on personality factors
   (d) males always have the power
   (e) females always have the power

14. The *stimulus-value-role theory, equity theory*, and *the principle of least interest* all have their roots in which theory?

   (a) structural-functionalism
   (b) conflict
   (c) symbolic-interactionism
   (d) exchange

15. People of the same age who marry each other is an example of:

   (a) hypergamy.
   (b) hypogamy.
   (c) exogamy.
   (d) the mating gradient.
   (e) endogamy.

16. Sociologists have defined the imbalance in the ratio of marriage-aged women and marriage-aged men as:

   (a) a marriage squeeze.
   (b) a marriage gradient.
   (c) hypergamy.
   (d) hypogamy.
   (e) exogamy.

17.   In most cultures, including the United States, informal norms encourage women to marry men of equal or higher social status. This is referred to as:

   (a)   hypogamy.
   (b)   the marriage gradient.
   (c)   the marriage squeeze.
   (d)   endogamy.

18.   *Propinquity* has to do with:

   (a)   age differences.
   (b)   racial and ethnic similarities.
   (c)   closeness in space.
   (d)   gender roles.
   (e)   religious differences.

19.   Which of the following is/are accurate concerning the *personal ads* taken out by women and men?

   (a)   Men offered financial security much more than women did.
   (b)   Women defined or offered themselves as attractive partners more than men.
   (c)   Men requested photographs more often than women.
   (d)   All of the above.

20.   According to a variety of sources, an average of _____ *percent* of high school and college students experience physical violence at some point in their dating relationships.

   (a)   25
   (b)   15
   (c)   80
   (d)   65
   (e)   4

21.   Why do teen victims of dating violence remain in their relationships?

   (a)   There might be the fear of being alone.
   (b)   Denial of the situation.
   (c)   There is often a feeling of loyalty or pity.
   (d)   Shame or embarrassment.
   (e)   All of the above.

22.   Concerning *date rape* and *acquaintance rape*:

   (a)   most rapes are date or acquaintance rapes.
   (b)   most reported rapes are stranger rapes.
   (c)   the younger the woman, the more likely that she knows the rapist.
   (d)   date and acquaintance rape cut across race, social class, and sexual orientation,
           and can be found in all geographic regions.
   (e)   all of the above.

Matching

a. functions of dating
b. exogamy
c. homogamy
d. propinquity
e. marriage gradient
f. endogamy
g. sex ratio
h. date rape

i. courtship
j. marriage squeeze
k. stimulus-value-role theory
l. pool of eligibles
m. principle of least interest
n. hypergamy
o. filter theory
p. dowries

1.   A rule governing mate selection and marriage with a particular group. ____
2.   The tendency for women to marry upward. ____
3.   The population of people our society has defined as acceptable marriage partners for us. ____
4.   The number of men for every 100 women. ____
5.   Socialization, recreation, mate selection, status grading and achievement. ____
6.   A social rule governing mate selection and marriage outside a particular group. ____
7.   Denotes closeness in place and space. ____
8.   An imbalance in the ratio of marriage-aged women to marriage-aged men. ____
9.   Relates to men marrying down and women marrying up, thus giving men at the top a larger field of eligibles. ____
10. The tendency to meet, date, and marry someone very similar to ourselves in terms of important or desirable characteristics. ____
11. Rape of a victim who is actually going out with the rapist. ____
12. Relates to a couple in which one partner is more committed to the relationship than the other, and the less committed partner trades her or his company for the other's acquiesce to his or her wishes. ____
13. A process of selecting a mate and developing an intimate relationship. ____
14. A popular version of the exchange theory of mate selection. ____
15. Sums of money or property brought to a marriage by a female. ____

Fill-In

1.   _____ refers to a process of pairing off that involves the open choice of mates and engagement in activities that allow people to get to know each other and progress through coupling and mate selection.
2.   Sociologists estimate that _____ *percent* of marriages in *India* are *arranged*.

3. In colonial New England, unmarried couples practiced _____, in which they spent the night wrapped in blankets or separated only by a wooden board down the middle of the bed.

4. The functions of dating (past and present) identified by G.N. Ramu include: _____, _____, _____, and _____.

5. _____ *socialization* refers to socialization that is directed toward learning future roles.

6. The _____ refers to the number of men to every 100 women.

7. According to researcher *Susan Basow's* application of *social-learning theory* to dating, women's scripts focus on enhancing their _____, making _____, and controlling _____ behavior.

8. Seldom are both parties equally interested in continuing a dating relationship. Thus, the one who is least interested has an advantage and is in a position to dominate. Some researchers have described this as the _____.

9. _____ are sums of money or property brought to a marriage by the female.

10. The people whom society has defined as *acceptable marriage partners* for us form what sociologists call a _____.

11. The opposite of *exogamy* is _____, or marriage within a particular group.

12. Several interrelated factors are discussed in the text as *limiting our pool of eligibles*, including the marriage _____ , the marriage _____, _____, _____, _____, _____, _____, _____ pressure.

13. The pattern of women marrying men of *lower social standing* than themselves is referred to as _____.

14. Sociologists will typically measure *social class* using a composite scale consisting of _____, _____, and _____.

15. _____ is used by sociologists to denote *closeness in place or space*.

16. Two important personal qualities that very critically affect *mate selection* are _____ and _____.

17. *Rape* is a behavior learned by men within a context of a _____ self-concept.

18. _____ are more likely than _____ to report feeling depressed, lonely, unhappy, and less free after a *breakup*.

Short-Answer

1. Briefly describe the custom of *arranged marriage* in nonindustrialized societies. What are the social functions served by an arranged marriage system?

2. Describe the current mate selection context in *China*. How are demographic conditions there affecting the relative status of women?

3. Briefly describe the historical mate selection customs of *keeping company* and *calling*.

4. In what important ways is *social class* related to mate selection?

5. What are the factors that limit or constrain our *pool of eligibles* in terms of mate selection? Describe how each of these factors is affecting you personally.

6. What are the advantages and risks of *cyberspace dating*?

7. Differentiate between *stimulus-value-role* and *equity* theories as examples of the exchange theory of mate selection.

8. What are five important points made by our authors concerning *date rape* and *acquaintance rape*?

9.   What are the differences in *personal ads* taken out by men and women? What factors do you think explain these differences?
10.   What are the similarities and differences between *gay and lesbian* mate selection patterns and *heterosexual* mate selection patterns.
11.   What are three important points being made by the authors regarding *African American lesbian* and *gay* dating?
12.   Describe the basic premise of *filter theory* regarding mate selection as a process.

PART VI: ANSWERS TO STUDY QUESTIONS

True-False

1.	T	(p. 113)	10.	T	(p. 123)
2.	T	(p. 113)	11.	T	(p. 124)
3.	T	(p. 113)	12.	T	(pp. 125-126)
4.	F	(p. 114)	13.	T	(p. 128)
5.	F	(p. 116)	14.	F	(p. 130)
6.	T	(p. 118)	15.	T	(p. 133)
7.	T	(p. 119)	16.	T	(p. 134)
8.	T	(p. 121)	17.	F	(p. 138)
9.	F	(p. 122)	18.	T	(p. 142)

Multiple-Choice

1.	b	(p. 112)	12.	c	(pp. 123-124)
2.	c	(pp. 112-113)	13.	b	(p. 125)
3.	d	(p. 113)	14.	d	(pp. 125-126)
4.	d	(p. 113)	15.	e	(p. 128)
5.	c	(p. 114)	16.	a	(p. 129)
6.	d	(p. 115)	17.	b	(p. 129)
7.	a	(p. 116)	18.	c	(p. 132)
8.	e	(pp. 118-119)	19.	d	(p. 135)
9.	b	(p. 119)	20.	a	(p. 140)
10.	b	(p. 120)	21.	e	(p. 141)
11.	e	(p. 121)	22.	e	(p. 142)

Matching

1.	f	(p. 128)	9.	e	(p. 130)
2.	n	(p. 130)	10.	c	(p. 128)
3.	l	(p. 128)	11.	h	(p. 142)
4.	g	(p. 120	12.	m	(p. 125)
5.	a	(pp. 118-119)	13.	i	(p. 113)
6.	b	(p. 128)	14.	k	(p. 125)
7.	d	(p. 132)	15.	p	(p. 127)
8.	j	(p. 129)			

Fill-In

1. Dating (p. 112)
2. 95 (p. 114)
3. bundling (p. 115)
4. socialization, recreation, status grading and achievement, mate selection (p. 118)
5. Anticipatory (p. 119)
6. sex ration (p. 120)
7. appearance, conversation, sexual (p. 121)
8. principle of least interest (p. 125)
9. Dowries (p. 127)
10. Pool of eligibles (p. 128)
11. Endogamy (p. 128)
12. Squeeze, gradient, race, social class, age, religion, sex and gender, propinquity, family and peer (pp. 128-132)
13. Hypogamy (p. 130)
14. Education, occupation, income (p. 131)
15. Propinquity (p. 132)
16. Attractiveness, companionship (p. 133)
17. Masculine (p. 143)
18. men, women (p. 143)

PART VII: IN FOCUS—IMPORTANT ISSUES

• Mate Selection in Cross-Cultural and Historical Perspective

Compare *mate selection* in the United States, China, and India was discussed in the text:

Describe *mate selection* in the United States for each of the following historical periods:

Colonial America

The 1920s and 1930s

Contemporary patterns

- The Intersections of Race, Gender, Class, and Sexual Orientation

    Identify two important points made by the authors for each of the following topics:

    Dating patterns among African Americans

    The impact of gender

    The impact of social class

    Lesbian and gay dating

- Theories of Mate Selection

    Describe each of the following theories:

    Exchange theories—

    stimulus-value-role theory

    equity theory

    Filter theories—

- Mate Selection: Finding and Meeting Partners

  Illustrate an example of how each of the following affects our pool of eligibles:

  marriage market

  marriage squeeze

  the marriage gradient

  race

  social class

  age

  religion

  sex and gender

  propinquity

  family and peer pressure

- Meeting Partners: Where and How

  Briefly discuss how each of the following will play a role, or has played a role in your mate selection process: school, church, and work, bars, personal ads, dating clubs and dating services, video dating, computer dating, dating in cyberspace

- The Future of Dating

  How do you think dating will be different for your children as compared to you?

- Violence In Dating and Intimate Relationships

  What are two important points being made about *dating violence* by our authors?

  What are five important facts being provided by the authors concerning *date rape* and *acquaintance rape*?

- Breaking Up

  What are the gender differences in terms of how people break up?

PART VIII: ANALYSIS AND COMMENT

- Applying the Sociological Imagination: "Choosing a Mate: A Content Analysis of Personal Ads" (p. 136)

  Key Points: Questions/Comments:

- In Other Places: "The Legitimation of Singlehood in Kenya" (p. 137)

  Key Points: Questions/Comments:

- Writing Your Own Script: Personal Biography and Social Structure: "Selecting a Mate" (p. 144)

  Key Points: Questions/Comments:

6 Sexuality and Intimate Relationships

PART I: CHAPTER OUTLINE

I. Human Sexuality: Past and Present
- A. Jewish Traditions and Human Sexuality
- B. Christian Traditions and Human Sexuality
- C. Sexuality in the United States: An Overview
- D. Sexual Attitudes and Behavior in the Twentieth Century

II. Sexuality As Social Learning
- A. Sources of Sexual Learning

III. Sexual Orientations
- A. Heterosexuality
- B. Homosexuality
- C. Bisexuality

IV. The Physiology of Sexuality
- A. The Sexual Response Cycle

V. Human Sexual Expression
- A. Autoeroticism
- B. Interpersonal Sexual Behavior
- C. Sexual Expression Among Lesbians and Gays

VI. Sexuality Across the Life Cycle
- A. Nonmarried Sexuality and Pregnancy
- B. Marital Sexuality: Does Good Sex Make Good Marriages?
- C. Extramarital Sexuality
- D. Postmarital Sexuality
- E. Sexuality and Aging
- F Women, Aging, and Sexuality

VII. Sexual Dysfunctions

VIII. Sexual Responsibility: Protecting Yourself From AIDS and Other STDs
- A. AIDS

IX. Summary

X. Key Terms

XI. Questions for Study and Reflection

XII. Further Reading

PART II: LEARNING OBJECTIVES

1. To be able to distinguish between sex and human sexuality.
2. To compare Ancient Jewish and early Christian traditions as they relate to human sexuality.
3. To consider historical trends in sexuality in the United States from Puritan time to the present.
4. To discuss the factors that contribute to our sexual identity, including significant others, the generalized other, schools, the mass media, and sexual scripts.
5. To begin to understand and discuss heterosexuality, homosexuality, and bisexuality as variations of human sexuality.
6. To be able to describe and discuss the physiology of human sexuality, particularly the sexual response cycle.
7. To be able to identify and discuss the different forms of autoeroticism.
8. To be able to identify and discuss interpersonal sexual behaviors.
9. To examine human sexuality across the life cycle.
10. To be able to identify and discuss the various types of sexual dysfunctions.
11. To be able to discuss AIDS and understand the importance of sexual responsibility.

PART III: KEY TERMS

AIDS

autoeroticism

bisexuality

climactric

coitus

cunnilingus

ejaculation

erogenous zone

erotic arousal

fellatio

generalized other

heterosexism

heterosexuality

homophobia

75

homosexuality

human sexuality

masturbation

menopause

nocturnal emissions

orgasm

petting

phallocentric

pleasuring

Puritan sexuality

refractory period

safe sex

sexual double standard

sexual dysfunction

sexually transmitted diseases

sexual orientation

sexual script

significant other

Victorian sexuality

wet dreams

PART IV: IMPORTANT RESEARCHERS

Allen Bell and Martin Weinberg   Philip Blumstein and Pepper Schwartz

Carol Darling   Sigmund Freud

John Gagnon and William Simon   Shere Hite

Morton Hunt   Alfred Kinsey

Simon LeVay   Linda Lindsay

William Master and Virginia Johnson   Adrienne Rich

PART V: STUDY QUESTIONS

True-False

1. As used in the text, the term *human sexuality* includes such behaviors as breast feeding, giving birth, and talking affectionately with someone. T F
2. According to *Ancient Jewish tradition*, a woman who was not a virgin at the time of marriage could be put to death. T F
3. As part of the *Christian tradition*, St. Paul believed that celibacy was superior to marriage and that all humans should strive for a chaste life. T F
4. At the base of the *Victorian view* of sexuality was the notion that any kind of sexual stimulation, especially orgasm, sapped a person's vital forces. T F
5. Recent survey results in the U.S. indicate that both women and men are having *more sex partners* today than during any other decade in this century. T F
6. According to NORC survey data, Americans report having sex (coitus) about two times per week, with single people having sex more often than married people. T F
7. *Marital status* has no impact on frequency of sexual activity in the United States. T F
8. According to psychoanalytic theorist *Sigmund Freud*, the *sex drive* is the motivation for all human behavior. T F
9. Regarding *gender differences* in sexuality, women think about sex more often than men do. T F
10. Research continues to show that both women and men in the Unites States accept a *double standard* regarding sexuality. T F

11. *Heterosexism* is a very strong force in the United States.   T F
12. Twin studies and research involving brain autopsies have shown some evidence for the *biological basis of homosexuality*.   T F
13. According to researcher *Alfred Kinsey*, the dichotomy of heterosexual versus homosexual may be misleading, arguing few of us are completely and exclusively heterosexual or homosexual.   T F
14. According to researchers *William Masters* and *Virginia Johnson*, the vagina, not the clitoris, is the central organ for orgasmic response in women.   T F
15. *Masturbation* is more common among people 18 to 24 years of age than are those who are 25 to 34 years of age.   T F
16. The practice of *oral sex* is more common among African Americans than among whites.   T F
17. Today, more than one-half of females and three-fourths of males aged 15-19 have experienced *sexual intercourse*.   T F
18. National survey research indicates that *extramarital sex* has increased since 1950, however may be decreasing since the mid-1980s.   T F
19. The majority of unmarried births are not to teenagers.   T F
20. Most divorced people do not become *sexually active* for three years following the divorce.   T F
21. According to research by *William Masters* and *Virginia Johnson*, about twenty percent of married couples in our society experience some kind of *sexual dysfunction*.   T F
22. Over ninety percent of males with AIDS are homosexual, bisexual, or intravenous drug users.   T F
23. AIDS infection rates is higher among African Americans and Hispanics than among whites.   T F
24. The most common way *women* are exposed to HIV is intravenous drug use.   T F
25. The *majority* of AIDS cases in the world are found in Europe and North America.   T F

Multiple-Choice

1. As used in the text, *sex* refers to:

   (a)   intercourse.
   (b)   genetic or biological sex.
   (c)   a wide range of sexual behaviors.
   (d)   all of the above.

2. *Human sexuality* refers to:

   (a)   the feeling, thoughts, and behaviors of humans.
   (b)   sexual intercourse and masturbation.
   (c)   breast-feeding.
   (d)   giving birth.
   (e)   all of the above.

3. During the *thirteenth century*, the church, through the writing of _____ renewed its position on sexuality as animalistic and an activity to be avoided.

   (a)   St. Thomas Aquinas
   (b)   St. Paul
   (c)   St. Augustine
   (d)   John Calvin

4.	*Victorian sexuality* was characterized by:

	(a)	a number of sexual taboos.
	(b)	the idea that sexuality was basically a male phenomenon.
	(c)	a prevailing belief that decent women did not experience a sexual desire.
	(d)	a differing set of norms based on gender.
	(e)	all of the above.

5.	Researcher *Carol Darling* divided this century into three major *ears* in terms of sexual behavior. The second major era, from the 1950s to 1970, is termed:

	(a)	the traditional period.
	(b)	the marriage context period.
	(c)	the permissive era.
	(d)	the era of permissiveness with affection.

6.	The *differing set of norms* based on gender is referred to as the sexual:

	(a)	orientation.
	(b)	tradition.
	(c)	double standard.
	(d)	script.

7.	*Sexual homogamy* refers to:

	(a)	having sexual partners who are very much like you in terms of race, education, socioeconomic level, age, and religion.
	(b)	being monogamous.
	(c)	having sex with a member of your own sex.
	(d)	having no particular sexual preferences.

8.	The *generalized other* refers to:

	(a)	the viewpoint of society at large.
	(b)	the opinions we have of our family.
	(c)	the biological side of our self.
	(d)	the sexual component of our self.
	(e)	cross-cultural influences on our society's norms and values.

9.	Which of the following have been identified as areas of *gender difference* in traditional *sexual scripting*?

	(a)	interest in sex is part of the male sexual script but not part of the female script
	(b)	males are expected to be the initiators and to take control of sexual activities
	(c)	females are expected to be submissive, conform, and give pleasure
	(d)	achievement and frequency is expected for males, but monogamy and exclusiveness is expected of females
	(e)	all of the above

10. *Heterosexism*:

(a)   is an extreme and irrational fear or hatred of homosexuals.
(b)   the belief that heterosexuality is the only right, natural, and acceptable sexual orientation.
(c)   the preference for sexual activities with a person of the other sex.
(d)   the preference for sexual activities with a person of the same sex.
(e)   male-centered sexuality.

11. *Homosexuality* refers to:

(a)   behavior.
(b)   identity.
(c)   sexual preference.
(d)   all of the above.

12. What is the *second phase* in *William Masters* and *Virginia Johnson's* sexual response cycle?

(a)   orgasm.
(b)   plateau.
(c)   resolution.
(d)   excitement.

13. Which of the following is *not* a form of *autoeroticism*?

(a)   erotic dreams
(b)   sexual fantasies
(c)   sexual intercourse
(d)   masturbation

14. Among men and women, the most common form of *sexual fantasy* involves:

(a)   using sexual devices.
(b)   penile-vaginal intercourse.
(c)   swapping partners.
(d)   multiple partners.
(e)   oral sex.

15. *Coitus* refers to:

(a)   penile-vaginal intercourse.
(b)   cunnilingus.
(c)   fellatio.
(d)   sexual fanatics.
(e)   extramarital sex.

16. Approximately what percentage of live births in the U.S. are to *unmarried women*?

    (a)   45
    (b)   33
    (c)   14
    (d)   21
    (e)   56

17. A *male climacteric* is most similar to female:

    (a)   frigidity.
    (b)   menstruation.
    (c)   arousal.
    (d)   menopause.

18. Each year approximately _____ *million people* are stricken with a *curable STDs*.

    (a)   10
    (b)   100
    (c)   333
    (d)   60

19. Experts estimate that approximately _____ people in the United States are infected with HIV.

    (a)   250,000
    (b)   1,500,000
    (c)   6,000,000
    (d)   740,000

20. Which of the following is accurate about AIDS?

    (a)   In the U.S. most people with AIDS are men.
    (b)   Although AIDS initially was identified with gays, the incidence of the disease is increasing among the sexually active heterosexual population.
    (c)   The intersection of age and race are clearly revealed in various AIDS statistics.
    (d)   Today, women are more likely than men to contract AIDS.
    (e)   All of the above are accurate about AIDS.

21. The World Health Organization estimates that _____ *million people* are infected with HIV worldwide.

    (a)   10.1
    (b)   20.2
    (c)   30.6
    (d)   81.7

Matching

a.	human sexuality	h.	Alfred Kinsey
b.	sexual double standard	i.	William Masters and Virginia Johnson
c.	sexual homogamy	j.	sexual arousal
d.	phallocentrism	k.	fellatio
e.	heterosexism	l.	coitus
f.	sexual orientation	m.	menopause
g.	homophobia	n.	sexual dysfunction

1. The belief that heterosexuality is the only right, natural, and acceptable sexual orientation. ____
2. Conducted research focusing on the physiology of sex. ____
3. When the menstrual cycle stops completely. ____
4. The differing set of norms based on gender. ____
5. An extreme and irrational fear or hatred of homosexuals. ____
6. Refers only to penile-vaginal intercourse. ____
7. Defining sexuality almost exclusively in terms of genital intercourse and male orgasm. ____
8. The inability to engage in or enjoy sexual activities. ____
9. Conducted research that found that a simple heterosexual-homosexual dichotomy does not exist in our society. ____
10. The stimulation or awakening of sexual desire that we feel ourselves or that we evoke in others. ____
11. Refers to feelings, thoughts, and behaviors of humans who have learned a set of cues that evoke a sexual or erotic response. ____
12. Involves not only whom one chooses as a sexual partner, but more fundamentally, the ways in which people understand and identify themselves. ____
13. The oral stimulation of the male genitals. ____
14. Choosing sexual partners who are very similar to us in terms of race, age, religion, socioeconomic level, and education. ____

Fill-In

1. In general terms _____ refers to feelings, thoughts, and behaviors of humans, who have learned a set of cues that evoke a sexual or an erotic response.
2. Ancient Jewish tradition placed great emphasis on _____ and _____.
3. Regarding the effects of gender on sexual behavior, our authors suggest women historically have experienced sexuality in terms of _____, _____, and _____.
4. The Protestant Reformation of the _____ *century* ushered in a diversity of views and attitudes concerning human sexuality.
5. The differing set of norms based on *gender* is referred to as the _____.
6. Approximately _____ of women in the U.S. have one *sexual partner (coitus)* in their lifetime.
7. Our authors suggest that perhaps the most alarming *gender difference* found in the NORC sex survey is the difference in female and male perception of what constitutes _____.
8. According to *Sigmund Freud*, the _____, which he viewed as a biologically determined force, is the motivator for all human behavior.
9. _____ involves not only whom one chooses as a sexual partner, but more fundamentally, the ways in which people understand and identify themselves. The four recognizable levels of *orientations* include: _____, _____, _____, and _____.

10. Social scientists, utilizing a *feminist perspective*, maintain that sexuality and sexual activities in the United States associated with a heterosexual orientation are _____--or male-centered, and are defined almost exclusively in terms of genital intercourse and male orgasm.

11. According to research by *William Masters* and *Virginia Johnson*, the *sexual response cycle* has four phases, including the _____, _____, _____, and _____.

12. _____ refers only to *penile-vagina intercourse*.

13. *Allen Bell* and *Martin Weinberg* have identified five *gay lifestyles*, including: _____, _____, _____, _____, and _____.

14. Research concerning *postmarital sexuality* cited in the text focuses on _____ people, _____, and _____.

15. As women age, their reproductive ability declines gradually. Somewhere around age 50, the *menstrual cycle* stops completely, marking _____.

16. The inability to engage in or enjoy sexual activities refers to _____.

17. Approximately _____ *percent* of women with AIDS are heterosexual and do not use intravenous drugs.

18. The two most common ways women are infected with *HIV* is _____ and by sexual contact with _____.

19. The majority of HIV/AIDS cases in the world today are found on the continents of _____ and _____.

20. *Safe sex* involves four basic components, including: (1) _____ about HIV prevention before having sexual relations, (2) being informed of what safe sex is and that it can be _____, (3) using _____ to protect yourself from potentially infected blood, semen, or vaginal fluids, and (4) avoiding _____, that could impair your ability to comply with the first three components.

Short-Answer

1. Distinguish between the concepts of *sex* and *human sexuality*.
2. Differentiate between *ancient Jewish* and *early Christian* traditions on human sexuality.
3. What are the two main points being stressed in this chapter about *human sexuality in Western society?*
4. Differentiate between *Puritan* and *Victorian* sexuality.
5. Identify five important findings from the human sexuality *surveys* reviewed in the chapter (NORC and Parade magazine surveys).
6. What is the picture being drawn of sexual attitudes and behaviors in the 1990s?
7. What role do you feel the *mass media* is playing in the social learning of sexuality?
8. What are the important gender difference in *sexual scripting* in our society?
9. According to the *Masters and Johnson* studies on the physiology of human sexuality, what are the four phases of the *sexual response cycle*? Briefly describe each.
10. What are the similarities between *heterosexuals, lesbians,* and *gays* in terms of sexual expression?
11. Generally describe how the expression of sexuality varies across the human life cycle, differentiating between women and men.
12. What are the *demographics of AIDS* in the United States? Globally?
13. What are the recommendations being made by the authors for preventing STDs and promoting *safe sex*?
14. What are the general demographic patterns of *teen pregnancy* in the U.S. today?

PART VI: ANSWERS TO STUDY QUESTIONS

True-False

1.	T	(pp. 148-149)	14.	F	(p. 169)
2.	T	(p. 149)	15.	F	(p. 171)
3.	T	(p. 150)	16.	F	(p. 173)
4.	T	(p. 151)	17.	T	(p. 174)
5.	F	(p. 154)	18.	T	(p. 177)
6.	F	(p. 154)	19.	T	(p. 177)
7.	F	(p. 154)	20.	F	(p. 178)
8.	T	(p. 158)	21.	F	(p. 180)
9.	F	(p. 160)	22.	T	(p. 184)
10.	T	(p. 160)	23.	T	(p. 184)
11.	T	(p. 163)	24.	T	(p. 186)
12.	T	(p. 164)	25.	F	(p. 187)
13.	T	(p. 168)			

Multiple-Choice

1.	b	(p. 148)	12.	b	(p. 16)
2.	e	(pp. 148-149)	13	c	(pp. 170-171)
3.	a	(p. 150)	14.	e	(p. 172)
4.	e	(p. 151)	15.	a	(p. 173)
5.	d	(p. 151)	16.	b	(p. 175)
6.	c	(p. 151)	17.	d	(p. 180)
7.	a	(p. 157)	18.	c	(p. 181)
8.	a	(p. 158)	19.	b	(p. 183)
9.	e	(p. 159)	20.	e	(pp. 184-185)
10.	b	(p. 163)	21.	c	(p. 187)
11.	d	(p. 164)			

Matching

1.	e	(p. 163)	8.	n	(p. 180)
2.	i	(p. 169)	9.	h	(p. 169)
3.	m	(p. 179)	10.	j	(p. 169)
4.	b	(p. 151)	11.	a	(p. 148)
5.	g	(p. 163)	12.	f	(p. 163)
6.	l	(p. 173)	13.	k	(p. 172)
7.	d	(p. 163)	14.	c	(p. 157)

Fill-In

1. human sexuality (p. 148)
2. marriage, reproduction (p. 149)
3. reproduction, oppression, vulnerability (p. 149)
4. sixteenth (p. 150)
5. sexual double standard (p. 151)
6. one-third (p. 155)
7. consensual sex (p. 157)
8. sex drive (p. 158)
9. Sexual orientation, heterosexuality, homosexuality, bisexuality, asexuality (p. 163)
10. phallocentric (p. 163)
11. excitement, plateau, orgasm, resolution (p. 169)
12. coitus (p. 173)
13. dysfunctional, functional, open-coupled, closed-coupled, asexual (p. 173)
14. divorced, widowed, widowers (p. 178)
15. menopause (p. 179)
16. sexual dysfunction (p. 180)
17. 39 (p. 184)
18. intravenous drug use, men (p. 186)
19. Africa, Asia (p. 187)
20. thinking and talking, pleasurable, barriers, drugs and alcohol (p. 188)

PART VII: IN FOCUS--IMPORTANT ISSUES

- Human Sexuality: Past and Present

    Compare *Jewish* and *Christian* traditions of human sexuality:

    Differentiate between *Puritan* and *Victorian* sexuality:

    What points are the authors making about whether or not a *sexual revolution* has occurred in the United States over the last thirty to forty years?

- Sexuality As Social Learning

    Differentiate between the male and female *sexual scripts* in our society:

- Sexual Orientations

    What is the evidence that *homosexuality* has a biological basis as a sexual orientation?

- The Physiology of Sexuality

    Identify and describe the four stages of the *sexual response cycle*:

- Human Sexual Expression

    Identify and define the three types of *autoeroticism* described in the text:

    What are three important points our authors make about sexual expression among *Lesbians* and *gays*:

- Sexuality across the Life Cycle

    Describe how *nonmarital pregnancy rates* have changed in the U.S. over the last half-century:

    What are two important points being made by our authors concerning:

    marital sexuality

    extramarital sexuality

    postmarital sexuality

    sexuality and aging

- Sexual Dysfunctions

    What is meant by the term *sexual dysfunction*?

    How common are sexual dysfunctions in the United States?

- Sexual Responsibility: Protecting Yourself from AIDS and other STDs

    What is AIDS? How is it transmitted?

    What are the *demographic* patterns of AIDS found around the world? In the United States?

    What are the four basic components of *safe sex*?

PART VIII: ANALYSIS AND COMMENT

- Applying the Sociological Imagination: "Human Sexuality in the Mass Media, Past and Present"
    Key Points: Questions/Comments:

- In Other Places: "Fishing at Lake Lovemaking"
    Key Points: Questions/Comments:

- Strengthening Marriages and Families: "Talking Frankly about Our Sexual Needs"
    Key Points: Questions/Comments:

- Writing Your Own Script: "Identifying Sexual Values"
    Key Points: Questions/Comments:

7 Nonmarital Lifestyles

PART I: CHAPTER OUTLINE

I.   Historical Perspectives
      A.   Singlehood in Early America
      B.   Singlehood in the Nineteenth and Early Twentieth Centuries
      C.   Singlehood Today: Current Demographic Trends

II.   Demystifying Singlehood
      A.   Individual Decision Making
      B.   The Influence of Social and Economic Forces
      C.   Types of Singles
      D.   Advantages and Disadvantages of Singlehood

III.   Single Lifestyles
      A.   Income
      B.   Support Networks
      C.   Life Satisfaction
      D.   The Never-Married in Later Life

IV.   Heterosexual Cohabitation
      A.   Historical Perspectives
      B.   The Meaning of Cohabitation Today
      C.   Reasons for Cohabitation
      D.   Advantages and Disadvantages of Cohabitation
      E.   Cohabitation and the Division of Labor
      F.   Cohabitation and Marital Stability
      G.   Cohabitation: International Perspectives
      H.   Cohabitation and the Law

V.   Lesbian and Gay Relationships
      A.   Methodological Issues
      B.   Demystifying Lesbian and Gay Relationships
      C.   Living Together: Domestic Tasks, Finances, and Decision-Making
      D.   The Social and Legal Context of Lesbian and Gay Relationships
      E.   Life Satisfaction: Elderly Lesbians and Gays

VI.   Communal Living
      A.   Advantages and Disadvantages of the Communal Lifestyle
      B.   Communes, Shared Housing, and the Future
      C.   Group Marriages

VII.   Summary

VIII.   Key Terms

IX.   Questions for Study and Reflection

X.   Further Reading

PART II: LEARNING OBJECTIVES

1. To gain historical perspective on singlehood as a lifestyle in the United States.
2. To begin to discuss and critique the stereotypes of singles, both in the past and in the present.
3. To identify and discuss the reasons why people remain single.
4. To identify and discuss the push and pull factors related to marriage and singlehood.
5. To identify and describe the different types of singles.
6. To discuss the relative advantages and disadvantages of remaining single.
7. To become aware of single lifestyles and issues of importance to this segment of our population across the life cycle.
8. To discuss the historical perspectives and the meaning of cohabitation today, including demographic trends—U.S. and Europe, reasons for cohabiting, types of cohabiting couples, advantages and disadvantages of cohabiting, and the legal aspects of this household structure.
9. To identify and discuss lesbian and gay single and cohabiting lifestyles.

PART III: KEY TERMS

cohabitation

common-law marriage

commune

domestic partnership

group marriage

palimony

push/pull factors

PART IV: IMPORTANT RESEARCHERS

Katherine Allen *—Never married Study of working-class women born 1910*

Philip Blumstein and Pepper Schwartz *Found that women do more housework*

Jaber Gubrium

Richard Higginbotham

Peter Kain

Pat Keith

Judy Rollins

Arthur Shostak

89

PART V: STUDY QUESTIONS

True-False

1. In this chapter, the term *single* refers only to never-married people.   T   F
2. The status of *singles* during colonial America was relatively high compared to single in our society today.   T   F
3. The view that marriages should be *happy* rather than merely a duty evolved gradually during the early nineteenth century.   T   F
4. A higher percentage of *whites*, females and males, remain single past age thirty than is the case for *African Americans* and *Latinos*.   T   F
5. Across all age categories over age eighteen, the percentage of single (never-married) men is *higher* than that of single women.   T   F
6. The percentage of *never-married adults* in our society is expected to rise over the next twenty years.   T   F
7. The population of singles in our society is described by the authors as being very homogenous.   T   F
8. According to the U.S. Census Bureau, most never-married people aged 18-24 *live with their parents*.   T   F
9. Research findings concerning how women and men develop support networks show that there are differences in terms of how we tend to value *friends*.   T   F
10. Historically, studies have shown married people to be *happier* and *more satisfied* with their lives than singles.   T   F
11. According to research findings by *Katherine Allen* and *Pat Keith*, aged, never-married singles tend to *live alone* and experience considerable *loneliness*.   T   F
12. *Unmarried-couple households* are defined by the Census Bureau as those households containing two unrelated adults of the opposite sex (one of whom is the householder) who share a housing unit with or without children under age fifteen present.   T   F
13. Research has found more *violence* in cohabiting couple households, especially young couple households, as compared to married couples.   T   F
14. There is significantly more *egalitarianism* within cohabiting couple households in terms of the division of labor than is found among married couple households.   T   F
15. Cohabitation is strongly related to marital success, with divorce rates among cohabiting couples who eventually marry being relatively low compared to their noncohabiting counterparts.   T   F
16. The U.S. has the *highest* rate of cohabitation in the world.   T   F
17. *Homosexual behavior* has existed throughout history and in every known culture.   T   F
18. As is found in heterosexual couple households, homosexual couple decision-making, like housework, is often related to income; that is, the partner with the higher income tending to have more power.   T   F
19. Lesbians and gays often keep their sexual orientation hidden because of fear of discrimination, ridicule, and harassment. For those who do "come out," typically the first person told is the homosexual's mother.   T   F
20. *Elderly homosexuals* tend to be poorly adjusted, isolated, and experience few life satisfactions compared with other lesbians and gays.   T   F

Multiple-Choice

1.   As used in this chapter, the term *single* means:

    (a)   never-married.
    (b)   widowed.
    (c)   separated.
    (d)   divorced.
    (e)   all of the above.

2.   In 1997, approximately thirty percent of men and twenty percent of women aged thirty to thirty-four were *single*. In 1890, comparable figures were:

    (a)   10/5
    (b)   27/15
    (c)   25/20
    (d)   5/10
    (e)   30/30

3.   According to the United States Census Bureau:

    (a)   the number of women and men who remain single into their late 30s has increased over the last thirty years.
    (b)   among both sexes, African Americans and Latinos have higher rates of singlehood than do their white counterparts.
    (c)   more African American men than women marry members of other racial or ethnic groups.
    (d)   the percentage of single men is higher than that of single women.
    (e)   all of the above.

4.   *Social and economic forces* as to why there are more singles today in our society include:

    (a)   the lessening of stigmas against singlehood.
    (b)   the lessening of the perceived benefits of marriage.
    (c)   economic facts such as staying in school longer to be able to get a better job, and more people being focused on their careers.
    (d)   the liberalization of sexual norms and the availability of contraceptive devices.
    (e)   all of the above.

5.   *Peter Stein* characterized factors which *attract* a person to a potential situation as:

    (a)   pushes.
    (b)   pulls.
    (c)   assets.
    (d)   magnets.
    (e)   draws.

6. As perceived by singles, which of the following is not identified as a relative advantage or disadvantage of singlehood?

    (a)   greater personal freedom
    (b)   more privacy
    (c)   less time to develop friendships
    (d)   financial independence
    (e)   loneliness and lack of companionship

7. Which of the following is *not* identified in the text as a type of *single lifestyle*?

    (a)   supportive
    (b)   passive
    (c)   activist
    (d)   residual
    (e)   social

8. The *median income* for female householders living alone (1996) was $16,398. The comparable figure for married couples with both spouses present was _____.

    (a) $34,678.
    (b) $67,358.
    (c) $49,858.
    (d) $26,986.

9. Approximately what percentage of people over the age of sixty-five are *never-married* singles?

    (a)   10.3
    (b)   6.9
    (c)   1.2
    (d)   15.0
    (e)   4.3

10. According to *Jaber Gubrium* which of the following is *not true* of elderly, never-married singles?

    (a)   they tend to be lifelong isolates
    (b)   they are lonely
    (c)   they are more positive than the widowed and divorced
    (d)   they evaluate every day in much the same way as their married peers
    (e)   all of the above

11. A cohabitative relationship that is based on the mutual consent of the persons involved, is not solemnized by a ceremony, and is recognized as valid by the state, refers to:

    (a)   covertive.
    (b)   palimony.
    (c)   common-law marriage.
    (d)   marriage.

12. Approximately how many *unmarried-couple households* are there in the U.S. today?

    (a)   1.76 million
    (b)   4.13 million
    (c)   10.45 million
    (d)   2.67 million

13. Which of the following is *not accurate* regarding the demographic characteristics of *cohabitants*?

    (a)   the majority of cohabitants are between the ages of 25 and 44 years of age
    (b)   slightly over one-third of cohabitants have children under the age of 15 living with them
    (c)   cohabitants tend to be more educated than their married counterparts
    (d)   cohabitants are less likely than their married counterparts to identifiy with an organized religion
    (e)   cohabitants become sexually active at younger ages than their noncohabiting counterparts

14. Which of the following is *not accurate* regarding cohabitation:

    (a)   cohabiting couples are less likely than married couples to pool their financial resources.
    (b)   cohabiting couples, especially young couples, experience a higher rate of violent behavior than do married couples.
    (c)   the division of labor in cohabiting couple households is not much different from their married counterparts.
    (d)   cohabitation is a good predictor of marital success.
    (e)   all of the above are inaccurate.

15. Which of the following is/are *inaccurate* concerning global research on cohabitation?

    (a)   approximately twenty-five percent of couples in Sweden live together, and almost all couples live together before getting married
    (b)   in Denmark, eighty percent of the adult population has cohabited at some point in time
    (c)   France, Germany, and the Netherlands all have higher rates of cohabitation than the United States
    (d)   China has a very low rate of cohabitation, particularly in rural areas
    (e)   a-c are all inaccurate

16.   On average, cohabiting lasts _____ years.

       (a)   1.5
       (b)   5.6
       (c)   12.1
       (d)   8.2
       (e)   3.7

17.   *Robert Higginbotham* argues that we use a _____ model to study and understand *same-sex couples*.

       (a)   palimony
       (b)   friendship
       (c)   egalitarian
       (d)   deviant

18.   Regarding the social and legal context of *lesbian* and *gay* relationships, which of the following is/are accurate?

       (a)   research has found no significant differences between lesbians and gays and their heterosexual counterparts in terms of couple adjustment, feelings of attachment, caring, and intimacy
       (b)   lesbians and gays in long-term relationships are generally denied legal and financial benefits such as community property rights, insurance coverage, and tax breaks
       (c)   in contrast to heterosexual couples, when lesbian and gay partners break up they are more likely to maintain close relationships with one another
       (d)   the average length of a gay cohabiting relationship is longer than the average heterosexual cohabiting relationship
       (e)   all of the above are accurate

19.   A _____ refers to a group of people (single or married, with or without children) who live together, sharing many aspects of their lives.

       (a)   palimony
       (b)   domestic partnership
       (c)   commune
       (d)   common-law marriage

20.   A _____ is a marriage of at least four people, two female and two male, in which each partner is married to all partners of the opposite sex.

       (a)   commune
       (b)   endogamous family
       (c)   group marriage
       (d)   polygamous marriage

Matching

a. types of singles
b. advantages of singlehood
c. disadvantages of singlehood
d. single lifestyles
e. common-law marriage
f. palimony

g. domestic partnerships
h. the workplace
i. commune
j. advantages of communes
k. group marriage

1. A cohabitive relationship that is based on mutual consent of the persons involved, is not solemnized by a ceremony, and is recognized as valid by the state. _____
2. A major area in which gays and lesbians experience discrimination. _____
3. Voluntary, stable, voluntary temporary, involuntary temporary, involuntary stable. _____
4. Egalitarian, personalized, cooperative. _____
5. A payment similar to alimony and based on the existence of a contract (written or implied) between partners regarding aspects of their relationship. _____
6. Loneliness, lack of companionship, social disapproval of their lifestyle. _____
7. A marriage of at least four people, two women and two men, in which each partner is married to all partners of the opposite sex. _____
8. A group of people (single or married, with or without children) who live together, sharing many aspects of their lives. _____
9. A term referring to unmarried couples who live together and share household and financial responsibilities. _____
10. Supportive, passive, activists, individualistic, social, professional. _____

Fill-In

1. *Singles* in early America were often _____ to responsible families.
2. Sociologist *Peter Stein* has characterized psychological, social, cultural, and economic factors as a series of _____, or *negative factors* and _____, or *attractions* to a potential situation.
3. One gender-specific *disadvantage of being single* concerns issues of _____.
4. Although there is some overlapping of activities, six different *lifestyle patterns* have been observed among the single population over the age of thirty, including: _____, _____, _____, _____, _____, and _____.
5. In 1997, female householders living alone had a median income of $16,398; the comparable figure for males was $_____.
6. Referring to singles who live alone, both women and men value friends, but in somewhat different ways. Women concentrate on establishing close _____ bonds, whereas men focus more on sharing their _____ and their _____.
7. Two factors are particularly significant in helping to explain why married couple households have a higher *median income* than households of single people. First, many married couple households have more than one _____, and earnings differences may reflect a systematic bias against _____ in the workplace.

8.   According to research by *Jaber Gubrium, elderly singles* tend to be lifelong _____, they are not particularly _____, they _____ everyday life in much the same way their married peers do, and they avoid the desolation of _____.

9.   _____ refers to a cohabitive relationship that is based on the mutual consent of the persons involved, is not solemnized by a ceremony, and is recognized as valid by the state.

10.   There are approximately _____ million *unmarried-couple households* in the U.S. today.

11.   Just as many reasons are given for cohabitation, the relationship established by cohabiting couples vary in terms of _____ *needs* and *degree of* _____.

12.   _____ is a payment similar to alimony and based on the existence of a contract (written or implied) between the partners regarding aspects of their relationship.

13.   Domestic _____ is a term referring to unmarried couples who live together and share housing and financial responsibilities. Many such couples are gay or lesbian.

14.   *Richard Higginbotham* suggests that instead of using a *marriage model* for studying *same-sex relationships* we use a _____ *model*.

15.   A _____ refers to a group of people (single or married, with or without children) who live together, sharing many aspects of their lives.

PART VI: ANSWERS TO STUDY QUESTIONS

True-False

1.	T	(p. 193)	11.	F	(p. 203)
2.	F	(p. 193)	12.	T	(p. 204)
3.	T	(p. 194)	13.	T	(p. 207)
4.	F	(p. 195)	14.	F	(p. 208)
5.	T	(p. 195)	15.	F	(p. 209)
6.	T	(p. 196)	16.	F	(p. 209)
7.	F	(p. 197)	17.	T	(p. 210)
8.	F	(p. 200)	18.	T	(p. 212)
9.	T	(p. 201)	19.	T	(p. 213)
10.	T	(pp. 201-202)	20.	F	(p. 214)

Multiple-Choice

1.	a	(p. 193)
2.	b	(p. 194)
3.	e	(p. 195)
4.	e	(pp. 196-197)
5.	b	(p. 196)
6.	c	(p. 198)
7.	d	(pp. 199-200)
8.	c	(pp. 200-201)
9.	e	(p. 202)
10.	b	(p. 202)

11.	c	(p. 203)
12.	b	(p. 205)
13.	c	(pp. 205-206)
14.	d	(pp. 207-208)
15.	d	(p. 209)
16.	a	(p. 209)
17.	b	(p. 211)
18.	e	(p. 212)
19.	c	(p. 214)
20.	c	(p. 216)

Matching

1.	e	(p. 203)
2.	h	(p. 214)
3.	a	(p. 197)
4.	j	(p. 214)
5.	f	(p. 209)

6.	c	(p. 198)
7.	k	(p. 216)
8.	i	(p. 214)
9.	g	(p. 210)
10.	b	(p. 198)

Fill-In

1. disposed (p. 193)
2. pushes, pulls (p. 196)
3. safety (p. 198)
4. supportive, passive, activist, individualistic, social, professional (pp. 199-200)
5. 27,266 (p. 200)
6. emotional, interests, values (p. 201)
7. wage earner, singles (p. 201)
8. isolates, lonely, evaluate, bereavement (p. 202)
9. Common-law marriage (p. 203)
10. 4.1 (p. 205)
11. individual, commitment (p. 207)
12. Palimony (p. 209)
13. Partnerships (p. 210)
14. Friendship (p. 211)
15. Commune (p. 214)

PART VII: IN FOCUS—IMPORTANT ISSUES

- Historical Perspectives

   What was the relative status of *single people in early America* compared to their married counterparts?

   In what important ways was singlehood different in the nineteenth and early twentieth centuries as compared to today?

   What are four important demographic facts about singlehood in our society today?

- Demystifying Singlehood

   Identify the important *individual decision making and social and economic forces* related to the increasing numbers of singles in our society today:

   What are the four *types of singles* identified in the text?

   Identify four advantages and four disadvantages of being single:

- Single Lifestyles

   What are the six different *lifestyle patterns of singles* identified in the text? Describe or illustrate each.

   Identify and describe three important factors that influence people living as singles:

   What are the general characteristics of *never-married* aged people in our society?

- Heterosexual Cohabitation

  What are the current *demographic trends* of cohabitation in our society?

  What are five general categories of people who most represent cohabiting couples today?

  What are three major reasons why people cohabitate?

  What are the relative *advantages* and *disadvantages* of cohabitation?

  How does cohabitation affect *gender role behavior* and *marital stability*?

- Lesbian and Gay Relationships

  In what important ways are gay and lesbian cohabiting couples different than their heterosexual counterparts? In what ways are they similar?

- Communal Living and Group Marriage

  What are the relative advantages and disadvantages of *communal living*?

PART VIII: ANALYSIS AND COMMENT

- In Other Places: "Certification of Single Women" (p. 198)

    Key Points: Questions/Comments:

- Applying the Sociological Imagination: "What Went Wrong?" (p. 208)

    Key Points: Questions/Comments:

- Social Policy Issues: "Coming Out" (p. 213)

    Key Points: Questions/Comments:

- Searching the Internet: "The Farm….." (p. 215)

    Key Points: Questions/Comments:

- Writing Your Own Script: "The Marital Decision" (p. 216)

    Key Points: Questions/Comments:

8 The Marriage Experience

PART I: CHAPTER OUTLINE

I. Why Do People Marry?
    A. Sociological Perspective
II. The Meaning of Marriage
    A. Marriage as a Commitment
    B. Marriage as a Sacrament
    C. Marriage as a Legal Contract
    D. Some Legal Aspects of the Marriage Contract
III. Change and Continuity in the Meaning of Marriage
    A. Provisions of the Modern Contract
    B. The Marriage Contract Today
    C. The Wedding
IV. Marriage and Gender
    A. "Her" Marriage
    B. "His" Marriage
V. Transitions and Adjustments to Marriages
    A. A Typology of Marital Relationships
VI. Heterogamous Marriages
    A. Interracial Marriages
    B. Interethnic Marriages
    C. Interfaith Marriages
VII. Marital Satisfaction, Communication, and Conflict Resolution
VIII. Summary
IX. Key Terms
X. Questions for Study and Reflection
XI. Further Reading

PART II: LEARNING OBJECTIVES

1. To review and discuss research findings concerning why people marry.
2. To be able to describe the meaning of marriage from both emotional and legal perspectives.
3. To discuss the meaning of marriage from a historical perspective.
4. To begin to explain how gender affects marriage, particularly marital satisfaction.
5. To discuss different wedding ceremonies found around the world.
6. To identify and describe different types of marriage.
7. To identify and discuss the demographic patterns found in our society regarding heterogamous marriages.
8. To consider the importance of communication and conflict resolution in marriage.

PART III: KEY TERMS

adultery

affinal relatives

bigamy

conjugal rights

coverture

heterogamous marriage

legal marriage

marital adjustment

personal marriage agreement

prenuptial agreement

principle of legitimacy

sacrament

social marriage

PART IV: IMPORTANT RESEARCHERS

Jessie Bernard   John Cuber and Peggy Herrof

John Gottman   Susan and Clyde Hendrick

Rushworth Kidder   Nicholas Kristof

Jeanette and Robert Lauer   Bronislaw Malinowski

Judy Pearson   Virginia Sapiro

Carl Weiser   Lenore Weitzman

PART V: STUDY QUESTIONS

True-False

1. The Methodist Church is the only Protestant denomination in the U.S. to formally recognize *same-sex marriages* as sacred unions. T F
2. Cross-cultural research on the institution of marriage has found that couples in *Japan* have a relatively *low level of compatibility* compared to couples in other nations around the world. T F
3. *Structural-functional theory* has been a dominant point-of-view in sociology for explaining why people marry while focusing on society's need or demand for the *legitimacy of children*. T F
4. The *feminist perspective* challenges the principle of legitimacy argument. T F
5. Research on the relationship between *marital commitment* and marital stability has found little evidence of a strong correlation. T F
6. Most people in the U.S. who marry for the first time do so under the auspices of some religious figure such as a Priest, Rabbi, or Minister. T F
7. Most researchers have found that *commitment* is a key factor in any intimate, emotionally satisfying, and meaningful marriage relationship. T F
8. *Social marriage* is a legally binding agreement or contractual relationship between two people that is defined and regulated by the state. T F
9. The most important marriage laws are *state laws*. T F
10. The U.S. was the first nation to legalize *same-sex marriages*. T F
11. Although the state Supreme Court had previously ruled that bans against same-sex marriages were unconstitutional, in 1998 voters amended the State Constitution to allow lawmakers to limit marriage to opposite-sex couples. T F
12. The typical state *age requirement* for marriage with parental consent in the United States is sixteen years of age. T F
13. *Blood tests* are required in all fifty states before a couple may get married. T F
14. The provisions of the modern marriage contract are similar to those based on the old principle of *coverture*. T F
15. *Conjugal rights* pertain to inheritance issues involving siblings. T F
16. Research by *Jessie Bernard* has found very high levels of similarity in how wives and husbands evaluate their marriages. T F
17. Studies have shown that wives are twice as likely as their husbands to say they *would marry* the same person again. T F
18. *Vital* and *total marriages* are classified as *intrinsic* marriages, because they appear to be rewarding in and of themselves to the couple. T F
19. *Heterogamous* marriages are less common today then they were in previous historical periods within our society. T F

20.   While the *divorce rate* has leveled off in recent years, almost two-thirds of the marriages entered into in recent years are expected to end in divorce or separation.   T   F

21.   According to *John Gottman*, the real reason marriages succeed or fail is really very simple: couples who stay together are *nice* to each other more often than not.   T   F

Multiple-Choice

1.   Which of the following do Americans rank at the *top* of their list of *sources of satisfaction*?

(a)   wealth
(b)   fame
(c)   good marriage
(d)   good health
(e)   satisfying work

2.   The single most important reason that people give for *getting married* is that they:

(a)   want financial stability.
(b)   want a companion.
(c)   want to secure their social standing.
(d)   are in love.

3.   *Rushworth Kidder* asked couples why they married or what they thought marriage offered. Their answers most frequently focused on:

(a)   commitment and sharing.
(b)   fun and excitement.
(c)   having children.
(d)   financial security.

4.   The *principle of legitimacy*--the notion that all children ought to have a legally recognized father--was first put forth by:

(a)   Emile Durkheim.
(b)   Jessie Bernard.
(c)   Nepoleon Chagnon.
(d)   Tom Seaver.
(e)   Bronislaw Malinowski.

104

5. Almost universally, *marriage* is based on the official control of:

   (a) wealth.
   (b) childbearing.
   (c) ideas.
   (d) society.
   (e) sex.

6. Approximately _____ *percent* of people in the U.S. will marry at least once in their lives.

   (a) 85
   (b) 90
   (c) 74
   (d) 99

7. According to recent estimates, approximately _____ of *first-time marriages* take place within the context of some type of religious ceremony.

   (a) one-half
   (b) three-fourths
   (c) one-eighth
   (d) two-thirds

8. According to the text, the most important *marriage laws* are _____ laws.

   (a) state
   (b) federal
   (c) local
   (d) international

9. In how many states in the United States can people of the *same-sex* marry?

   (a) 0
   (b) 50
   (c) 14
   (d) 5
   (e) 26

10. *Cohabitation* and *common-law marriage* are both examples of:

   (a) legal marriage.
   (b) social marriage.
   (c) sacred marriage.
   (d) residual marriage.

11. In 1989, _____ became the first country to legalize *same-sex unions.*

    (a)   the United States
    (b)   Japan
    (c)   Singapore
    (d)   Denmark
    (e)   Austria

12. In every state except one (Georgia) the legal age at which marriage can be contracted *without parental consent* is:

    (a)   14
    (b)   16
    (c)   12
    (d)   15
    (e)   18

13. *Affinal relatives* are related by:

    (a)   blood.
    (b)   adoption.
    (c)   marriage.
    (d)   same-sex parent.

14. Which of the following have been incorporated into *modern marriage laws* in the United States?

    (a)   the wife is responsible for caring for any children
    (b)   the husband is the head of the household
    (c)   the wife is responsible for caring for the home
    (d)   all of the above
    (e)   none of the above

15. Wedding planning experts estimated that the average cost of a wedding in the U.S. in 1997 was:

    (a) $10,000.
    (b) $6,000.
    (c) $40,000.
    (d) $27,000.
    (e) $17,000.

16. The degree to which a couple get along with each other or have a good working relationship and are able to satisfy each other's needs over the marital life course refers to:

    (a)   marital adjustment.
    (b)   marital success.
    (c)   marital happiness.
    (d)   marital quality.

17. Which *type of marriage relationship* involves little conflict but also little passion and attention to each other?

   (a)   total
   (b)   devitalized
   (c)   conflict-habituated
   (d)   passive-congenial

18. Approximately what percentage of marriages today are *interracial*?

   (a)   2
   (b)   5
   (c)   3
   (d)   1

19. *John Huber* and *Peggy Harroff* identified different types of marriages representing a wide-range of communication patterns and interaction styles. Three of these were labeled as conflict-habituated, devitalized, and passive-congenial. These authors categorized these as:

   (a)   intrinsic marriages.
   (b)   failed marriages.
   (c)   closed-marriages.
   (d)   behavioral marriages.
   (e)   utilitarian marriages.

20. According to *John Gottman*, the four most *destructive behaviors* to marital happiness are:

   (a)   fear, hatred, avoidance, and rejection.
   (b)   criticism, contempt, defensiveness, and stonewalling.
   (c)   withdrawal, violence, jealousy, and envy.
   (d)   dependence, denial, acceptance, and projection.

Matching

a.	social marriage	g.	personal marriage agreement
b.	bigamy	h.	prenuptial agreement
c.	fornication	i.	marital adjustment
d.	affinal relatives	j.	intrinsic marriages
e.	coverture	k.	utilitarian marriages
f.	conjugal rights	l.	heterogamous marriage

1. A written agreement between a married couple in which issues of role responsibility, obligation, and sharing are addressed in a manner that is tailored to their own personal preferences, desires, and expectations. _____
2. People related by marriage. _____
3. The degree to which a couple get along with each other or have a good working relationship and are able to satisfy each other's needs over the marital life course. _____

4. Marrying one person while still being married to another. ____
5. Marriages appearing to be rewarding. ____
6. Marriages between people who vary in certain social and demographic characteristics. ____
7. Rights pertaining to the marriage relationship. ____
8. Marriages appearing to be based on convenience. ____
9. A relationship between people who cohabit and engage in behavior that is essentially the same as within a legal marriage, but without engaging in a marriage ceremony that is validated by the state. ____
10. Sexual intercourse outside legal marriage. ____
11. The idea that a wife is under the protection and influence of her husband. ___
12. An agreement developed and worked out in consultation with an attorney and filed as a legal document. ____

Fill-In

1. In addition to *love* and *commitment* in the United States, a number of other _____ and _____ reasons motivate people to *marry*.
2. The _____ is the notion that all children ought to have a socially and legally *recognized father*.
3. From a religious perspective, *marriage* is regarded as a _____, or a sacred union or rite.
4. *Jeannette* and *Robert Lauer* found that a key factor contributing to the longevity of a relationship is the belief in marriage as a long-term _____ and _____ institution.
5. _____ and _____ marriage are examples of *social marriage*.
6. In addition to requiring _____ in marital relationships, marriage law also requires _____.
7. _____ *relatives* are people related by marriage.
8. *Blood tests* are required in many states to determine _____.
9. In the past, *age restrictions for marriage* were tied to the question of _____, whereas today the concern is _____.
10. The *common-law concept* of _____ is the idea that a wife is under the protection and influence of her husband.
11. In *China* the _____ is an ancient custom that is being revived. It ensures that everyone may have a partner in the afterlife.
12. Among the *Tiwi* of Australia, there is no such thing as a _____.
13. A _____ is a written agreement between a married couple in which issues of role responsibility, obligation, and sharing are addressed in a manner that is tailored to their own personal preferences, desires, and expectations.
14. _____ is the degree to which a couple get along with each other or have a good working relationship and are able to satisfy each others' needs over the marital life course.
15. *John Cuber* and *Peggy Harroff* identified five distinct types of marriages, representing a wide range of communication patterns and interaction styles. These included the _____ *marriage*, the _____ *marriage*, the _____ *marriage*, the _____ *marriage*, and the _____ *marriage*.
16. _____ *marriage* refers to marriages between people who vary in certain social and demographic characteristics.

17.	Research has consistently found that married people, compared to unmarried people, report being _____, _____, and generally more_____ with their lives.

18.	Three essential characteristics of *successful marriages* are _____ *communication*, _____-disclosure, and *conflict and* _____ *resolution.*

19.	*John Gottman* argues that couples that stay together are _____ to each other. Further, couples who are satisfied with their relationships maintain a _____-to-one ratio of positive to negative moments in their relationship.

20	According to *John Gottman* the four most *destructive behaviors* to marital happiness are _____, _____, _____, and _____.

Short-Answer

1.	What are the major reasons given by people in the United States as to *why they marry*?
2.	Cross-culturally, how does the United States rank in terms of survey results on *marital compatibility*? What factors are important for marital compatibility in other countries?
3.	Differentiate between the *legal, social,* and *sacred* meanings of marriage.
4.	What points are being made by the authors concerning the *legal aspects of marriage*?
5.	Review the major points being made in the text concerning the *legal gender bias* in marriage laws in the United States--both historically and today.
6.	What are the conclusions about marriage being made by *Jessie Bernard*?
7.	What are the important demographic facts in our society today concerning *heterogamous marriage*?
8.	What seem to be the important determinants of *marital satisfaction* in our society today?
9.	What are the most significant aspects of meaningful *conflict and conflict resolution* in marriage relationships?

PART VI: ANSWERS TO STUDY QUESTIONS

True-False

1.	F	(p. 218)	12.	F	(p. 226)
2.	T	(p. 220)	13.	F	(p. 227)
3.	T	(p. 221)	14.	T	(p. 228)
4.	T	(p. 221)	15.	F	(p. 229)
5.	F	(p. 222)	16.	F	(p. 236)
6.	T	(p. 222)	17.	F	(p. 236)
7.	T	(p. 222)	18.	T	(p. 238)
8.	F	(p. 223)	19.	F	(p. 238)
9.	T	(p. 223)	20.	T	(p. 249)
10.	F	(p. 224)	21.	T	(p. 249)
11.	T	(p. 225)			

Multiple-Choice

1.	c	(p. 219)	11.	d	(p. 224)
2.	d	(p. 219)	12.	e	(p. 226)
3.	a	(p. 219)	13.	c	(p. 226)
4.	e	(p. 221)	14.	d	(p. 228)
5.	b	(p. 221)	15.	e	(p. 235)
6.	c	(p. 222)	16.	a	(p. 237)
7.	b	(p. 223)	17.	b	(p. 237)
8.	a	(p. 223)	18.	b	(p. 238)
9.	a	(p. 223)	19.	e	(p. 238)
10.	b	(p. 224)	20.	b	(p, 247)

Matching

1.	g	(p. 233)	7.	f	(p. 229)
2.	d	(p. 223)	8.	k	(p. 238)
3.	i	(p. 237)	9.	a	(p. 223)
4.	b	(p. 226)	10.	c	(p. 223)
5.	j	(p. 238)	11.	e	(p. 228)
6.	l	(p. 238)	12.	h	(p. 233)

Fill-In

1. social, economic (p. 220)
2. principle of legitimacy (p. 221)
3. sacrament (p. 222)
4. commitment, sacred (p. 222)
5. Cohabitation, common-law (p. 223)
6. heterosexuality, monogamy (p. 226)
7. Affinal (p. 226)
8. the presence of STDs (p. 227)
9. reproduction, maturity (p. 227)
10. coverture (p. 228)
11. spirit wedding (p. 231)
12. unmarried female (p. 231)
13. personal marriage agreement (p. 233)
14. Marital Adjustment (p. 237)
15. conflict-habituated, devitalized, passive-congenial, vital, total (pp. 237-238)
16. Heterogenous (p. 238)
17. happier, healthier, satisfied (p. 243)
18. effective, self, conflict (pp. 244-247)
19. nice, 5 (p. 247)
20. criticism, contempt, defensiveness, stonewalling (p. 216)

PART VII: IN FOCUS--IMPORTANT ISSUES

- Why Do People Marry?

  Identify the top six reasons people give for getting married:

  How do *functionalists* and *feminists* differ in their understanding of the principle of legitimacy?

- The Meaning of Marriage

  Define each of the following three perspectives on marriage:

  marriage as a commitment

  marriage as a sacrament

  marriage as a legal contract

  Discuss the legal aspects of marriage as they relate to *heterosexuality* and *monogamy*:

  Discuss the legal aspects of marriage as they relate to *gender*:

- Change and Continuity in the Meaning of Marriage

  Identify the major provisions of the *modern marriage contract*:

  What are the major points being made by the authors concerning *weddings* in the U.S. today?

- Marriage and Gender

  Differentiate between *his* and *her* marriage:

- Transitions and Adjustments to Marriages

  Identify and describe the five *types of marriage* reviewed in the text:

- Heterogamous Marriages

  Identify three important demographic facts concerning each of the following:

  interracial marriages

  interethnic marriages

  interfaith marriages

- Marital Satisfaction, Communication, and Conflict Resolution

  What is meant by *marital success*?

  What are the important components of *effective communication*?

  What role does *self-disclosure* play in marital success and quality?

  What are the important qualities of *conflict and conflict resolution* in a marital or intimate relationships?

PART VIII: ANALYSIS AND COMMENT

- In Other Places: "Marriage Traditions and Rituals in the United States" (pp. 230-231)

  Key Points: Questions/Comments:

- Searching the Internet: "Typical Spending for a Medium-Size Wedding, 1997" (p. 235)

  Key Points: Questions/Comments:

- Family Profile: "Laurel and Ralph Kemp" (p. 241)

  Key Points: Questions/Comments:

- Strengthening Marriages and Families: "Communication, Conflict Resolution, and Problem Solving In Marriages and Intimate Relationships" (p. 246)

  Key Points: Questions/Comments:

- Writing Your Own Script: "Preparing Your Relationship Contract" (pp. 248-249)

  Key points: Questions/Comments:

9 Reproduction and Parenting

PART I: CHAPTER OUTLINE

I.   Historical Overview: Fertility Trends in the United States
     A.   Current Fertility Patterns
II. To Parent or Not?
     A.   The Costs of Parenthood
     B.   The Benefits of Parenthood
     C.   The Social Pressures to Procreate
     D.   The Child-Free Option
     E.   Delayed Parenthood
III. Controlling Fertility
     A.   Historical Perspectives
     B.   Race, Class, and Age
     C.   Reasons for Not Using Contraceptives
IV. Abortion
     A.   Public Attitudes Toward Abortion
V.   Infertility
     A.   Causes of Infertility
     B.   Consequences of Infertility
VI. Reproduction without Sex: The New Technologies
VII. The Choice to Parent
VIII. Conception
     A.   Multiple Conception and Births
     B.   Sex Preference and Selection
IX. Pregnancy
     A.   Prenatal Development and Care
     B.   Prenatal Problems and Defects
X.   Expectant Fathers
     A.   The Cultural Double Bind
XI. Parental Adjustments, Adaptations, and Patterns of Child Rearing
     A.   Parental Roles
     B.   Gender Differences in the Experience of Parenthood
     C.   Styles of Parenting
     D.   Race and Class
     E.   Lesbian and Gay Parents
     F.   Single Parents
     G.   Teenaged Parents

PART II: LEARNING OBJECTIVES

1.   To be able to define and illustrate important concepts used in the analysis of demographic patterns in society.
2.   To consider the historical trends in fertility in the United States.
3.   To outline the costs and benefits of being a parent.
4.   To identify factors affecting the decision by married couples to remain childless.
5.   To consider the issue of fertility control, and define contraception and analyze the pattern of contraceptive use in the United States.
6.   To provide a historical overview of the abortion issue.
7.   To identify and describe the new technologies available for facilitating the birth of a child.
8.   To define and discuss issues related to conception, pregnancy, and prenatal care.
9.   To identify and describe issues related to becoming a parent, differentiating between those most relevant to the father and those most relevant to the mother.
10.   To identify and discuss the adjustments involved in becoming a parent.
11.   To identify and discuss the relative advantages and disadvantages of several different parenting styles.
12.   To identify and discuss issues related to lesbian and gay parents, single parents, and teenage parents.

PART III: KEY TERMS

abortion

amniocentesis

antinatalist attitude

artificial insemination

conception

congenital

contraception

couvade

embryopathy

embryo transplant

fertility

fertility rate

fetal alcohol syndrome

infertility

in vitro fertilization

midwife

morbidity

mortality

motherhood mystique

ovulation

postnatal depression

pronatalist attitude

sonogram

surrogacy

total fertility rate

ultrasound

zygote

PART IV: IMORTANT RESEARCHERS

Diane Baumrind   David Blankenhorn

Jerry Burger and Linda Burns   Patricia Hill Collins

Martin Faux   Sigmund Freud

Nancy Gibbs   Joan Huber

Melvin Kohn   David Popenoe

Margaret Sanger   Jarrold Shapiro

Murray Strauss   Margaret Usdansky

PART V: STUDY QUESTIONS

True-False

1. *Fertility* refers to the actual number of live births in a population.   T   F
2. *Latinas* have higher fertility rates than other women in the United States.   T   F
3. *China's one-child policy* is an example of an *antinatalist force*.   T   F
4. *Margaret Sanger* coined the term *birth control* as a positive description of family limitations.   T   F
5. Most pregnancies in the U.S. are *unintended* (the result of accidents).   T   F
6. Most women in the U.S. who have an *abortion* are under the age of twenty-five.   T   F
7. The *Hyde Amendment* provided for federal funds for poor women's birth control needs and costs.   T   F
8. About seventy-five percent of *infertility* is traced solely to the male partner.   T   F
9. *Artificial insemination* refers to surgically removing a woman's eggs and fertilizing them in a petri dish with a partner's or donor's sperm.   T   F
10. *Conception* refers to the process by which a male sperm cell penetrates a woman's ovum.   T   F
11. *Amniocentesis* involves a procedure whereby a fertilized egg from one woman is surgically removed and then implanted into an infertile woman.   T   F
12. Regardless of their causes, all defects present at birth are referred to as *congenital*.   T   F
13. Not only is *smoking* detrimental to the health of the smoker, it also has been shown to be detrimental to the health of the fetus. This is the case whether the smoker is the father or the mother.   T   F

14. The *cultural double bind* refers to the dilemma faced by women because of the conflicts between the motherhood mystique and the changing gender roles in our society. T F
15. The *couvade* refers to the postpartum sex taboo for women. T F
16. The traditional notion of fatherhood emphasizes the *instrumental role*. T F
17. In 1997, there were almost three million *father-only* homes, a significantly higher number than was found back in 1970. T F
18. The *authoritative parenting style* encourages children to be autonomous and self-reliant, with parents generally relying on positive reinforcements, while avoiding punative and repressive methods of discipline. T F
19. *Gays* raising children tend to be more rigid and less nurturing in terms of gender role socialization and the gender division of household labor than heterosexual fathers. T F
20. Women and children in single-parent homes run about a fifty percent chance of living in *poverty*. T F
21. Most unwed mothers in the U.S. are *teenagers*. T F
22. The U.S. is virtually the only modern society with increasing rates of births to *unwed mothers*. T F

Multiple-Choice

1. The period between *1946 to 1965* has come to be known among demographers as the *baby _____ period.*

   (a) bust
   (b) strain
   (c) bullet
   (d) boom
   (e) echo

2. The *total fertility rate* in the U.S. today is approximately:

   (a) 1.5
   (b) 2.5
   (c) 2.0
   (d) 1.0
   (e) 2.9

3. In comparison to other racial and ethnic groups _____-*Americans* have the *lowest fertility rates.*

   (a) Asian
   (b) Latin
   (c) Native
   (d) African

118

4. According to the U.S. Census Bureau, most American women aged eighteen to thirty-four *expect to have* _____ *children.*

    (a) no
    (b) one or two
    (c) two or three
    (d) three or four
    (e) four or more

5. Approximately _____ *percent* of all married couples in the U.S. consciously and purposely choose to remain *child-free*.

    (a) 1
    (b) 5
    (c) 7
    (d) 10
    (e) 15

6. Several factors have contributed to the pattern of *delayed parenting*. Which of these is/ are *not a factor*?

    (a) improved contraceptives and new reproductive technologies
    (b) greater cultural acceptance of singlehood as a lifestyle
    (c) changes in gender expectations
    (d) apprehensiveness about the high divorce rate
    (e) all of the above

7. The battle to make *contraception* legal was ignited by _____, a public-health nurse in the early 1900s.

    (a) Elizabeth Cady Stanton
    (b) Ruth Benedict
    (c) Kristen Luker
    (d) Margaret Mead
    (e) Margaret Sanger

8. Approximately _____ *million* women become *pregnant* each year in the United States.

    (a) 2
    (b) 6
    (c) 4
    (d) 8
    (e) 3

9.   Approximately _____ *percent* of all pregnancies are terminated by *abortion.*

    (a)   10
    (b)   50
    (c)   20
    (d)   33
    (e)   15

10.   The *Hyde amendment* of 1976:

    (a)   legalized abortion.
    (b)   provided tighter regulations for surrogacy.
    (c)   prohibited federal Medicaid funds to be used for abortions except in cases where the woman's life is threatened.
    (d)   required minors to get parental permission to get married.
    (e)   enabled minors to get contraceptives without parental permission.

11.   At any given time, approximately _____ *percent* of all married couples in the U.S. experience some form of *infertility.*

    (a)   15 to 20
    (b)   30 to 40
    (c)   25 to 30
    (d)   5 to 10
    (e)   1 to 5

12.   About _____ *percent* of *fertility problems* are traced directly to the *male partner.*

    (a)   10
    (b)   20
    (c)   40
    (d)   90
    (e)   60

13.   *In vitro fertilization*:

    (a)   is a procedure whereby a fertilized egg from a woman donor is transplanted into a fertile woman.
    (b)   involves surgically removing a woman's eggs and fertilizing them in a petri dish with the partner's or donor's sperm.
    (c)   involves the injecting of sperm into the vagina or uterus of an ovulating woman.
    (d)   none of the above.

14.   The release of a mature egg refers to:

    (a)   a zygote
    (b)   ovulation
    (c)   amniocentesis
    (d)   artificial insemination

15. A *zygote* is:

    (a)   a male sperm.
    (b)   an infertile male.
    (c)   an infertile female.
    (d)   an unfertilized egg.
    (e)   a fertilized egg.

16. *Amniocentesis*:

    (a)   allows parents to see the fetus and any movements it makes.
    (b)   is a form of in vitro fertilization.
    (c)   is performed when there is some concern about hereditary disorders.
    (d)   produces a zygote.
    (e)   is a condition in which a male has a low sperm count due to excessive spitting and pants-hiking.

17. *Morbidity* refers to:

    (a)   death.
    (b)   illness.
    (c)   infertility.
    (d)   nutrition.

18. Researcher *Lee Shapiro* suggests that the pregnancy of a partner thrusts a man into an alien world. He refers to this as a:

    (a)   developmental lag.
    (b)   couvade.
    (c)   bundling condition.
    (d)   cultural double bind.
    (e)   coverture.

19. When expectant fathers develop symptoms similar to those of the pregnant woman, it is sometimes referred to as *sympathetic pregnancy*, or as:

    (a)   couvade.
    (b)   bundling.
    (c)   quickening.
    (d)   embryopathy.

20.   Which of the following is *not* part of the *motherhood mystique*?

(a)   the ultimate achievement and fulfillment of womanhood is through motherhood
(b)   the body of work assigned to mothers is contradictory and does not neatly fit together
(c)   to be a good mother, a woman has to enjoy being a mother and all the work that is defined as part of the mothering role
(d)   a woman's attitude about mothering affects her children

21.   Based on his review of the literature, researcher *Michael Lamb* identified three *fathering styles*. Which of the following is *not* one of the styles he identified?

(a)   engagement
(b)   accessibility
(c)   distal
(d)   responsibility

22.   *Parenting styles* that have been identified include:

(a)   authoritarian, permissive, authoritative.
(b)   responsible, caring, loving.
(c)   focal, connected, isolated.
(d)   holistic, comparative, situated.

23.   Which of the following statements is/are *correct*?

(a)   the number of single-parent families has increased dramatically over the past two decades in the United States
(b)   half of the children born today in the United States will likely live in a single-parent family before they reach adulthood
(c)   almost one-third of all births in the United States involve unwed mothers
(d)   the greatest increases in the rate of single childbearing occurred among college-educated, employed white women.
(e)   all of the above

24.   Women and children in single-parent homes headed by women continue to be at high risk for a life of poverty. The *rate of poverty* for this group is about _____ percent.

(a)   15
(b)   24
(c)   63
(d)   48

25.   _____ has a one percent rate of births to *unwed mothers*.

(a)   Sweden
(b)   Japan
(c)   France
(d)   England

Matching

a. fertility   g. zygote
b. contraception   h. amniocentesis
c. infertility   i. morbidity
d. artificial insemination   j. couvade
e. in vitro fertilization   k. instrumental role
f. ovulation   l. authoritative style

1. A fertilized egg. _____
2. Involves the injection of semen into the vagina or uterus of an ovulating woman. _____
3. A parenting style that encourages children to be autonomous and involving the use of positive reinforcements. _____
4. Mechanisms for preventing fertilization. _____
5. Relates illness in a population. _____
6. The traditional notion of fatherhood. _____
7. Involves surgically removing a woman's eggs, fertilizing them in a petri dish with the partner's or donor's sperm, and then implanting one or more of the fertilized eggs in the woman's uterus. _____
8. The actual number of live births in a population. _____
9. The release of a mature egg. _____
10. Performed when there is concern about hereditary disease. _____
11. The inability to conceive after twelve months of unprotected intercourse or the inability to carry a pregnancy to live birth. _____
12. Expected fathers developing a sympathetic pregnancy. _____

Fill-In

1. Demographers use the term _____ *rate* to refer to the number of births per thousand women of childbearing years (ages 15-44) in a given year.
2. _____--the actual number of live births in a population—is both a _____ and a _____ phenomenon.
3. By 1900, the *total fertility rate* had _____ to _____ that of a century earlier.
4. According to the U.S. Department of Agriculture, average new parents will spend _____ to raise a child from birth to the age of seventeen.
5. *Benefits of parenthood* identified in the text include: _____ bonds, _____ status, _____ and _____.
6. _____ refers to mechanisms for preventing fertilization.
7. _____ was the first state to *regulate abortion*. It did so in _____.
8. The medical profession defined *infertility* as the inability to conceive after _____ of unprotected intercourse.
9. The major causes of *female infertility* are failure to _____ and blockage of the _____.
10. _____ involves surgically removing a woman's eggs, fertilizing them in a petri dish with the partner's or donor's sperm, and then implanting one or more of the fertilized eggs in a woman's uterus.

11. In _____, a woman agrees to be artificially inseminated with a man's sperm, carry the fetus to term, and relinquish all rights to the child after it is born.

12. An _____ allows a physician and the couple to observe the developing fetus directly by viewing electronically the echoes of sound waves pulsating through the pregnant woman's body.

13. Research has shown repeatedly that experiences such as those of *race*, *age*, and *class* have important effects on _____ (illness) and _____ (death.)

14. When HIV infected babies are born they generally have prominent physical features—particularly involving facial features and the shape of the head. This *physical appearance* is referred to as _____.

15. On the one hand, men are encouraged to participate in the pregnancy and birth of their children; but on the other hand, they are treated as outsiders by everyone concerned. This has been referred to as the _____.

16. Research cited in the text suggests that when mothers work, fathers become more *engaged* and *accessible* but not more _____ for their children.

17. According to *Melvin Kohn*, the _____ or _____ *value orientation* is more commonly found among working-class and lower-class parents. In contrast, among middle-class parents, a _____ or _____ *value orientation* is more common.

18. Approximately _____ lesbian or *gay couples* are raising one or more children.

19. Almost _____ of all live births in the U.S. are to *unwed mothers*.

20. Although many and complex factors account for different rates of *unmarried births around the world*, two important factors are believed to be the different levels of _____ use and rates of _____ pregnancy between countries.

Short-Answer

1. How have *fertility rates* changed in the U.S. over the last 200 years (generally)? What factors over the generations have most influenced these rates?

2. What are the current fertility patterns in the U.S. by *race, ethnicity*, and *age*.

3. What are the relative *costs* and *benefits* of parenthood?

4. What are some of the reasons why married couples choose to remain *child-free*?

5. What are the major *methods of fertility control*? Describe each.

6. What are five reasons why sexually active people *do not use* contraception?

7. Discuss *abortion* in historical perspective.

8. What is *infertility*? What are its causes?

9. Identify and describe the *new reproductive technologies* reviewed in the text. What are the moral, legal, and social issues involved with each of these technologies?

10. What is *conception*? Describe this event physiologically.

11. Discuss *pregnancy and prenatal development* as presented in the text. What are the prenatal care recommendations being made in the text?

12. What are the major *prenatal problems* (defects)? What are their causes?

13. What is meant by the terms *cultural double bind*? What evidence can you offer that this phenomenon occurs in our society?

14. What are the major concerns of *expectant fathers*?

15. What are the components of the *motherhood mystique*?

16. Discuss the issue of *gender differences* in the experience of parenthood.

17. What are the major *parental adjustments* after the birth of a child?

PART VI: ANSWERS TO STUDY QUESTIONS

True-False

1.	T	(p. 253)	12.	T	(p. 268)
2.	T	(p. 254)	13.	T	(p. 269)
3.	T	(p. 257)	14.	F	(p. 272)
4.	T	(p. 258)	15.	F	(p. 272)
5.	T	(pp. 258-259)	16.	T	(p. 275)
6.	T	(p. 259)	17.	T	(p. 277)
7.	F	(p. 260)	18.	T	(p. 279)
8.	F	(p. 261)	19.	F	(p. 283)
9.	F	(p. 262)	20.	T	(p. 285)
10.	T	(p. 265)	21.	F	(p. 286)
11.	F	(p. 267)	22.	F	(p. 286)

Multiple-Choice

1.	d	(p. 252)	14.	b	(p. 265)
2.	c	(p. 253)	15.	e	(p. 265)
3.	c	(p. 254)	16.	c	(p. 267)
4.	b	(p. 254)	17.	b	(p. 268)
5.	c	(p. 256)	18.	d	(pp. 271-272)
5.	e	(p. 257)	19.	a	(p. 272)
6.	e	(p. 257)	20.	b	(p. 274)
7.	e	(p. 258)	21.	c	(p. 278)
8.	b	(p. 258)	22.	a	(p. 279)
9.	d	(p. 259)	23.	e	(p. 284)
10.	c	(p. 260)	24.	d	(p. 285)
11.	a	(p. 261)	25.	b	(p. 286)
12.	c	(p. 261)			
13.	d	(pp. 262-263)			

Matching

1.	g	(p. 265)	7.	e	(p. 262)
2.	d	(p. 262)	8.	a	(p. 253)
3.	l	(p. 279)	9.	f	(p. 265)
4.	b	(p. 258)	10.	h	(p. 267)
5.	i	(p. 268)	11.	c	(p. 261)
6.	k	(p. 275)	12.	j	(p. 272)

Fill-In

1. fertility (p. 253)
2. Fertility, biological, social (p. 253)
3. declined, half (p. 253)
4. 149,820 (p. 255)
5. emotional, adult, fun, enjoyment (pp. 255-256)

6. Contraception (p. 258)
7. Connecticut, 1821 (p. 260)
8. 12 months (p. 261)
9. ovulate, fallopian tubes (p. 261)
10. In vitro fertilization (p. 262)
11. surrogacy (p. 263)
12. ultrasound (p. 267)
13. morbidity, mortality (p. 268)
14. embryopathy (p. 271)
15. cultural double standard (p. 272)
16. responsible (p. 278)
17. traditional, conformity, developmental, self-direction (p. 279)
18. one million (p. 283)
19. one-third (p. 284)
20. contraceptive, teenage (p. 286)

PART VII: IN FOCUS—IMPORTANT ISSUES

- Historical Overview: Fertility Trends in the United States

Generally describe the *fertility patterns* for different racial, ethnic, and age categories as presented in Table 9.1 and Figure 9.2 (p. 254)

- To Parent or Not?

What are the *costs of parenthood*?

What are the *benefits of parenthood*?

Provide two example of *antinatalist forces* and two examples of *pronatalist forces*:

- Controlling Fertility

Referring to Appendix D, identify and describe the major *birth control methods* available in our society today:

Identify and describe three *methods of abortion* as reviewed in Appendix C:

- Infertility

  Identify three *causes of infertility:*

- Reproduction Without Sex: The New Technologies

  Define each of the following reproductive technologies:

  Artificial insemination

  In vitro fertilization

  Embryo transplant

  Surrogacy

- The Choice to Parent

  Identify one major point being made in this section of the chapter:

- Conception

  What points do the authors make about *sex preference and selection*?

- Pregnancy

  Identify four major *prenatal problems or defects*. What are their causes?

- Expectant Fathers

  What is the *cultural double bind*?

- Parental Adjustments, Adaptations, and Patterns of Child Rearing

  What are the basic parts of the *motherhood mystique*?

What are four different views of *fatherhood* identified in the chapter?

What are the major *gender differences* in the experience of parenthood?

Identify and describe the three basic *styles of parenting*:

Summarize in the paragraph the patterns of parenting found in each of the following categories:

African Americans:

Latinas/os:

Native Americans:

Asian Americans:

Teenage fathers:

Teenage mothers:

Single Parents:

PART VIII: ANALYSIS AND COMMENT

- Social Policy Issues: "Protecting Fetal Rights" (p. 270)

    Key Points: Questions/Comments:

- Family Profile: "The Typak Family" (p. 273)

  Key Points: Questions/Comments:

- In Other Places: "Shared Paternity" (p. 278)

  Key Points: Questions/Comments:

- Writing Your Own Script: "To Parent or Not?" (p. 288)

  Key Points: Questions/Comments:

10 Evolving Work And Family Structures

PART I: CHAPTER OUTLINE

I. The Transformation of Work and Family Roles
    A. Reasons Women Work
II. Work and Family Structures
    A. Traditional Nuclear Families
    B. The Two-Person Career
    C. Dual-Earner Families
    D. Commuter Marriages
III. The Impact of Work On Family Relationships
    A. Marital Power and Decision Making
    B. Marital Happiness
    C. Husbands and the Division of Household Labor
    D. Child Care
IV. Integrating Work and Family Life: Resolving Role Conflict
    A. Strategies for Conflict Resolution
V. Inequalities in the Workplace: Consequences for Families
    A. Occupational Distribution
    B. The Race-Gender Gap in Earnings: Good News and Bad News
    C. Sexual Harassment
VI. The Economic Well-Being of Families
    A. Who Are the Poor?
    B. Unemployment and Underemployment
    C. Homelessness
    D. The Welfare Debate
VII. Restructuring the Workplace
    A. Workplace Changes
    B. Family Leave
VIII. Summary
IX. Key Terms
X. Questions for Study and Reflection

PART II: LEARNING OBJECTIVES

1. To be able to describe the changing composition of the U.S. labor force during the last century, and particularly over the last twenty-five years.
2. To consider the transition in U.S. families from the traditional nuclear family to the two-income family.

3.   To analyze the impact of work on family relationships.
4.   To identify and evaluate strategies for conflict resolution within families, especially those with two spouses/parents working outside of the home in paid employment.
5.   To identify and discuss inequalities in the workplace and their consequences for families.
6.   To become aware of some demographic characteristics of unemployment and underemployment in our society.
7.   To identify and discuss the demographics of poverty and the impact of welfare reform on the poor.
8.   To discuss the problem of homelessness in our society.
9.   To consider how the workplace and society can be restructured to accommodate the changing needs of families in the United States.

PART III: KEY TERMS

Aid to Dependent Children

commuter marriage

comparable worth

Family and Medical Leave Act

Family Support Act

feminization of poverty

flextime

job sharing

labor force participation rate

occupational distribution

Pregnancy Discrimination Act of 1978

role conflict

role overload

sexual harassment

spillover effects

underemployment

working poor

PART IV: IMPORTANT RESEARCHERS

Ruben Hill   C. Wright Mills

Katerine Newman and Chauncy Lennon   Karen Pyke

Peter Rossi   Beth Shelton

Felice Schwartz   Patricia Voydanoff

PART V: STUDY QUESTIONS

True-False

1.   *Labor force participation rates* among women in the United States are actually higher today than among men.   T F
2.   *Labor force participation rates* refers to the percentage of workers in a particular group who are employed or who are actively seeking employment.   T F
3.   Prior to World War II, the majority of *women workers* in the U.S. were young, single, poor, and women of color.   T F
4.   Over the next five years the projected *labor force participation rate* for African American women is expected to be considerably higher than for white women.   T F
5.   According to the U.S. Department of Labor, the majority of women work for the same reason men do-- *to support themselves and their families*.   T F
6.   For *men*, the difference in labor force participation rates are more pronounced across race and ethnicity than is true for women.   T F
7.   Most surveys in the U.S. reveal a clear pattern that wives and husbands both would prefer a *traditional homemaker* at home if possible.   T F
8.   One of the most consistent findings relating to the impact of work on family life deals with the relationship between *income* and *power* in decision making.   T F
9.   According to the U.S. Labor Department, in about thirty percent of *dual-earner families* the wife makes more than her husband.   T F
10.   Research findings on the relationship between marital happiness and dual-earner couples has been *inconsistent*.   T F
11.   Among men who are employed full-time in the labor force, *whites*, as compared to *African Americans* and *Latinos*, spent the most time in such tasks as cooking, cleaning, and caring for children.   T F

12. *Felice Schwartz* suggested that employers divide women into two groups based on whether they are *career-primary* or *family-and-career women*, calling this latter notion the *mommy-track*. T F

13. The median full-time, year-round earnings for *minority women* are higher than for their *white women* counterparts. T F

14. *Sexual harassment* includes unwanted leers, comments, and suggestions, and is not limited to unwanted physical contact of a sexual nature. T F

15. Race, socioeconomic status, sexual orientation, age, and marital status do not seem to affect the experience of *sexual harassment* in our society. T F

16. Approximately twenty percent of all U.S. families are classified as being *poor*. T F

17. Most poor families have at least one person *employed* in the labor force. T F

18. Over two-thirds of the *homeless population* in the U.S. today is comprised of *women and their dependent children*. T F

19. Rates of homelessness are greater among *African Americans* than among *whites*. T F

20. Until 1993, the U.S. was one of the few industrialized societies that *did not* have a national *family-leave policy*. T F

Multiple-Choice

1. Today, approximately ___*percent of men* aged sixteen yeas of age and older are in the labor force.

   (a) 55
   (b) 85
   (c) 75
   (d) 65
   (e) 92

2. In 1997, the labor force participation rate for *white women* was 59.5 percent. For *black women* the rate was _____ percent

   (a) 46.2
   (b) 37.4
   (c) 28.9
   (d) 81.7
   (e) 61.3

3. The highly idealized family structure consisting of a working husband, a full-time homemaker, and at least one child under the age of eighteen, currently represented _____ *percent of all households* in the United States.

   (a) 14
   (b) 25
   (c) 20
   (d) 7
   (e) less than 1

4. Today's *dual-earner couples* constitute approximately _____ *percent* of all married couples and cut across all class and ethnic lines.

   (a)   70
   (b)   50
   (c)   20
   (d)   90
   (e)   40

5. When both spouses work there is a tendency for:

   (a)   men to have more power in family decision making.
   (b)   women to have more power in decision making.
   (c)   more equality between the spouses in family decision making.
   (d)   there to be no difference in decision making compared to traditional single breadwinner families.

6. According to the Census Bureau, which of the following is the single most important *cause of resentment* among married women?

   (a)   money
   (b)   how much her mate helps around the house
   (c)   pets
   (d)   disciplining children
   (e)   problems with relatives

7. Today, approximately _____ *percent* of employed women with a child under the age of five uses *organized day care*.

   (a)   60
   (b)   15
   (c)   42
   (d)   29
   (e)   6

8. _____ occurs when a person occupies two different roles that involve contradictory expectations of what should be done at a given time.

   (a)   Role conflict
   (b)   Role Strain
   (c)   Role exit
   (d)   Occupational distribution

9.   Which of the following is/are identified in the text as *strategies* for conflict resolution in families?

      (a)   establishing priorities within the home and workplace
      (b)   exiting one of the roles
      (c)   making the role conflict public and demanding changes either within the family or within the larger society
      (d)   all of the above
      (e)   none of the above

10.   In 1997, what percentage of the U.S. work force was represented by *women*?

      (a)   25
      (b)   37
      (c)   46
      (d)   54

11.   On average in the United States today, employed women earn _____ *percent* of what men earn.

      (a)   46
      (b)   74
      (c)   96
      (d)   86

12.   In 1996, the *median family income* for married-couple families in which the wife did not work was $33,748. The comparable figure for married-couple families in which both spouses worked was:

      (a) $81,032.
      (b) $67,341.
      (c) $42,759.
      (d) $37,493.
      (e) $58,381.

13.   In 1997, the *official poverty level* for a family of four in the U.S. was:

      (a) $21,981.
      (b) $27,318.
      (c) $9,673.
      (d) $16,400.

14.   The official *unemployment rate* in the U.S. today is approximately _____ percent.

        (a)   5
        (b)   1
        (c)   3
        (d)   9
        (e)   13

15.   Examples of *underemployment* includes:

        (a)   involuntary part-time employment.
        (b)   full-time workers who make very little money.
        (c)   workers with skills greater than required by their current job.
        (d)   all of the above.
        (e)   none of the above.

Matching

a.	labor force participation rate	h.	46.3
b.	two-person marriage	i.	comparable worth
c.	commuter marriage	j.	pay equity
d.	29	k.	$16,400
e.	role conflict	l.	flextime
f.	role overload	m.	59.8
g.	occupational distribution	n.	$21,300

1.   Percentage of mothers of preschool children under the age of five who use organized day care arrangements. _____
2.   Refers to the location of workers in different occupations. _____
3.   The principle of equal pay for different jobs of similar worth. _____
4.   The percentage of workers in a particular group who are employed or who are actively seeking employment. _____
5.   The federal government's poverty level for a family of four. _____
6.   A situation in which a person's various roles carry more responsibilities than that person can reasonably manage. _____
7.   Arrangements which allow employees to choose when they arrive at and leave work--within limits. _____
8.   Occurs when a person occupies two different roles that involve contradictory expectations of what should be done at a given time. _____
9.   Dual-earner couples who maintain separate residences in different geographical locations. _____
10.   The percentage of all females over the age of fourteen in the labor force. _____
11.   The percentage of the work force who are female. _____
12.   A work pattern which incorporates the wife into her spouses job. _____

Fill-In

1. Negative _____ *effects* involve bringing home the problems and stresses experienced at work.

2. Approximately 75.9 percent of *white men* are in the labor force. The comparable rate for *black men* is _____ percent.

3. One variation of the traditional nuclear family/work relationship is the _____ *career* which incorporates the wife into her spouse's job through the expectation that she will be available to entertain his business associates, engage in volunteer activities that will enhance his organization's image, attend company parties and other events, socialize with her husband's coworkers off the job, and, at the same time, attend to the children and keep the household functioning smoothly.

4. Today, about _____ *percent* of married-couple families are *dual-earner families*.

5. The impact of work on family relationships is significant. Four important points are discussed in the text concerning these impacts include *marital* _____ and _____ *making*, *marital* _____, *husbands and the* _____, and _____.

6. A national opinion poll showed, next to money, how much my mate _____ is the single biggest cause of resentment among married women or cohabiting women.

7. Recent national research has found that working mothers spent *3.3 hours* on chores during work days and *5.8 hours* on chores on non-work days. The comparable figures for working husbands are _____ hours and _____ hours.

8. Regardless of the type of *child-care arrangements* in use, the majority of families who need child care confront two major problems: _____ and _____.

9. *Felice Schwartz* proposed that employers divide women into two groups based on whether they are *career-primary* or *career-and-family* women. This latter category Felice Schwartz called the _____.

10. Concerning the integration of work and the family, *strategies for conflict resolution* in families include: establishing _____, _____ one of the roles, and making the _____ public and demanding changes either within the family or within the larger society.

11. Three issues of special significance in the workplace that point to *inequalities between the sexes* concern occupational _____, the gender gap in _____, and _____.

12. _____ refers to the principle of equal pay for different jobs of similar worth.

13. In 1996, the median family income for *dual-earner* married couple families was _____.

14. In 1996, the median family income for *white families* was _____, for *African American families* _____, and for *Latina/os families* _____.

15. The increase in the number of women and children among the *poor* is referred to as the _____.

16. Children under the age of eighteen account for _____ *percent of the poor*.

17. *Peter Rossi* has identified two categories of *homeless people*: the _____ and the _____.

18. *Single adult males* account for _____ *percent of the homeless population* in our society.

19. The Personal Responsibility and Work Opportunity Reconciliation Act of 1996, also know as the Welfare Reform Act, has several provisions. Two of the most significant ones are a _____ *requirement* mandating two years of assistance with a five year cap on the total time a family can receive assistance, and significant reductions in the _____ *program*.

20.   Approaches to changing the *workplace* to make it easier for *working parents* to balance family and employment include: companies providing permanent _____ *employment with benefits,* _____ , and _____ *arrangements.*

Short-Answer

1.   What were the major *transformations in the workforce* in the U.S. during the twentieth century?
2.   What are three major reasons why so many more *women are working* outside the home today in our society?
3.   Differentiate between *commuter marriages* and *two-person careers.* Would you consider participating in either? Why or why not?
4.   What are the relative advantages and disadvantages of the status of *housewife* (for the wife, the husband, and the family)?
5.   What is the impact of work on *marital power* and *decision making*?
6.   What is the relationship between dual-earner marriages and *marital happiness*?
7.   Review the research data and conclusions on these data concerning the *division of household labor* for dual-earner families.
8.   What are the patterns in *child care arrangements* for dual-earner families? What are some of the problems confronted by such families?
9.   Identify three types of *underemployment.*
10.   What are the three issues related to *inequalities in the workplace* that are identified in the text? Provide evidence for each of these.
11.   What is the current *poverty level* for a family of four in the United States? Develop a budget for a family of four using this household income level.
12.   What are the *demographics of poverty* in the U.S. today?
13.   What are the major components of *welfare reform* in our society today?
14.   What are the *demographics of homelessness* in our society today? What factors influence the rate of homelessness?
15.   What are three *recommendations* being made in the text for *restructuring the workplace*? What other recommendations do you have to improve the relationship between the workplace and the family?
16.   What are the *strategies for conflict resolution* as discussed in the text? Briefly describe each of these.

PART VI: ANSWERS TO STUDY QUESTIONS

True-False

1.	F	(p. 292)	11.	F	(p. 300)
2.	T	(p. 293)	12.	T	(p. 301)
3.	T	(p. 293)	13.	F	(p. 304)
4.	F	(p. 293)	14.	T	(p. 305)
5.	T	(p. 293)	15.	F	(p. 305)
6.	T	(p. 293)	16.	F	(p. 306)
7.	F	(p. 294)	17.	T	(p. 307)
8.	T	(pp. 297-298)	18.	F	(p. 311)
9.	T	(p. 298)	19.	T	(p. 311)
10.	T	(p. 298)	20.	T	(p. 315)

Multiple-Choice

1.	c	(p. 293)	9.	d	(pp. 302-303)
2.	e	(p. 293)	10.	c	(p. 304)
3.	d	(p. 294)	11.	b	(p. 304)
4.	a	(p. 296)	12.	e	(p. 306)
5.	c	(p. 297)	13.	d	(p. 306)
6.	a	(p. 299)	14.	a	(p. 308)
7.	d	(p. 301)	15.	d	(pp. 309-310)
8.	a	(p. 302)			

Matching

1.	d	(p. 301)	7.	l	(p. 314)
2.	g	(p. 303)	8.	e	(p. 302)
3.	i	(p. 305)	9.	c	(p. 296)
4.	a	(p. 293)	10.	m	(p, 293)
5.	k	(p. 306)	11.	h	(p. 304)
6.	f	(p. 299)	12.	b	(p. 295)

Fill-In

1. spillover (p. 292)
2. 61.3 (p. 293)
3. two-person (p. 295)
4. 70 (p. 296)
5. power, decision, happiness, division of household labor, child care (pp. 297-300)
6. helping around the house (p. 299)
7. 2.1, 4.9 (p. 299)

8. high cost, limited availability (p. 301)
9. mommy track (p. 301)
10. priorities, exiting, role conflict (pp. 302-303)
11. distribution, pay, sexual harassment (pp. 304-305)
12. Comparable worth (p. 305)
13. $58,381 (p. 306)
14. $44,756, $26,522, $26,179 (p. 306)
15. feminization of poverty (p. 307)
16. 40 (p. 307)
17. literally homeless, precariously housed (p. 310)
18. 45 (p. 311)
19. work, Food Stamp (p. 312)
20. part-time, job sharing, flextime (p. 314)

PART VII: IN FOCUS--IMPORTANT ISSUES

- The Transformation of Work and Family Roles

    During the twentieth century, what has been the general pattern of employment rates for women and men?

    What are the major reasons for why more women are working in the paid labor force?

- Work and Family Structures

    Define and provide demographic patterns for the following family and work structure:

    traditional nuclear family

    the two-person career

    dual-earner families

    commuter marriages

- The Impact of Work on Family Relationships

    What is the impact of work on *marital power*?

    What is the impact of work on *marital happiness*?

    How is the *division of household labor* affected by working wives and mothers?

    For single-parent families with a mother or father working in the labor force, or for dual-earner families with children, what are the primary *child-care arrangements* of preschoolers?

    What is the *mommy track*? What do you think about this system?

- Integrating Work and Family Life: Resolving Role Conflict

    Identify and define the three *strategies for conflict resolution*:

- Inequalities in the Workplace: Consequences for Families

    What is the "bad news" and what is the "good news" about the *race-gender gap earnings*?

- The Economic Well-Being of Families

    What is meant by the *feminization of poverty*? What is the evidence that it exists in our society?

Why are low *unemployment rates* misleading as an indicator of how well our families are doing economically? How do unemployment rates vary by *age, race,* and *ethnicity*?

What are the major cause of *homelessness* in our society?

What exactly is the *Welfare Reform Act*? What are its effects on society?

- Restructuring the Workplace

    What are three recommendations being made in the text for improving the relationship between the workplace and the family?

PART VIII: ANALYSIS AND COMMENT

- Family Profile: "The Schlichting Family" (p. 295)

    Key Points: Questions/Comments:

- Social Policy Issues: "Is Welfare Reform Working?" (p. 313)

    Key Points: Questions/Comments:

- Writing Your Own Script: "Work/Family Decisions" (p. 315)

  Key Points: Questions/Comments:

- Searching the Internet: "The 10 Best Companies for Working Mothers" (p. 316)

  Key Points: Questions/Comments:

11   Violence and Abuse

PART I: CHAPTER OUTLINE

PART II: LEARNING OBJECTIVES

1. To discuss the concept of family violence from historical and cross-cultural perspectives.
2. To discuss the prevalence of violence in U.S. culture.
3. To identify and refute common myths about violence and abuse.
4. To discuss in detail the social problem of woman battering.
5. To describe the myths and realities of rape in U.S. society.
6. To review evidence concerning the victimization of women within our criminal justice system.
7. To identify and describe the effects of and responses to abuse.
8. To discuss the prevalence and causes of child abuse, child sexual assault, sibling abuse, and elder abuse in U.S. society.
9. To consider the various explanations offered by researchers as to why these various types of violence occur so often in our society.

PART III: KEY TERMS

battered-child syndrome

battered-woman syndrome

elder abuse

incest

infanticide

rape syndrome

sexual assault

victim blaming

woman battering

PART IV: IMPORTANT RESEARCHERS

Mary Daley pg. 320, 396   David Finkelhor and Keerti Yllo

Henry Kempe pg. 343   David Levinson

Erin Pizzey   Samual Radbill

Suzanne Steinmetz   Lenore Walker

PART V: STUDY QUESTIONS

True-False

1. Approximately ninety-five percent of the adult victims of domestic violence in the United States are *women*. T F
2. Research focused on in the text shows that family violence is a *uniquely American* phenomenon that has come into being only in recent generations. T F
3. Approximately one-half of all *murdered women* in the United States are killed by a current or former partner. T F
4. According to the authors, the pervasiveness of sex and violence toward women in the *media* acts to desensitize both men and women to the seriousness and unacceptability of violence against human beings. T F
5. *Cohabiting* women are more likely to be victims of battering than married women. T F
6. According to the authors, a common reason why women stay in violent relationships is *love*. T F
7. The Department of Justice estimates that nine percent of *rape and sexual assault victims* in the United States are *males*. T F
8. *Rape* is the most frequently committed violent crime in the United States, and the least reported of all violent crimes. T F
9. Most police calls for battering result in an *arrest*. T F
10. Most women who fight back against their abuser and kill them are convicted and sent to jail. T F
11. Most offenders who commit violent crimes against children are *women*. T F
12. According to the U.S. Census Bureau, less than fifteen percent of *child abuse and neglect victims* are between the ages of six and thirteen. T F
13. The term *child sexual abuse*, as defined in the text, refers to the use of a child for the sexual gratification of an adult. T F
14. Research indicates that among children who abuse their parents, the most frequent offenders are adult *sons*. T F
15. *Sibling violence* is higher among children living in families in which child and spouse assault also occur. T F

Multiple-Choice

1. According to *David Levinson's* analysis of cross-cultural data on family violence which of the following is the most common form of *family violence*?

    (a)   child abuse
    (b)   wife beating
    (c)   sibling abuse
    (d)   elder abuse

2. Not until the _____ was *wife beating* banned in the United States.

    (a)   1880s
    (b)   1970s
    (c)   1950s
    (d)   1920s

3. Approximately _____ of all *murders* in the United States are perpetrated by one family member against another.

    (a)   one-fifth
    (b)   one-tenth
    (c)   one-sixth
    (d)   one-third
    (e)   one-half

4. By the time most U.S. children reach the age of eighteen they have witnessed more than _____ *television murders*.

    (a)   30,000
    (b)   20,000
    (c)   40,000
    (d)   90,000

5. Approximately eleven percent of all reported *criminal assault cases* are aggravated assaults between _____.

    (a)   husbands and wives
    (b)   siblings
    (c)   parents and their dependent children
    (d)   adults and their dependent parents

147

6.   *Violence* is the reason stated for divorce in _____ *percent* of middle-class marriages.

   (a)   10
   (b)   22
   (c)   41
   (d)   56

7.   Most researchers today classify *battering* in terms of:

   (a)   frequency.
   (b)   intention.
   (c)   dependency.
   (d)   severity.

8.   For women, approximately two-thirds of violent victimizations are committed by someone known to them: husbands, boyfriends, acquaintances, or other relatives. In contrast, victimization by intimates and other relatives accounts for only _____ *percent* of all violence against men.

   (a)   1
   (b)   10
   (c)   5
   (d)   18

9.   *Marital rape* has been classified into different categories. Which of the following was *not* identified in the text as one of these categories?

   (a)   force-only
   (b)   battering rape
   (c)   obsessive rape
   (d)   abusive rape

10.   What percentage of rape victims ever see their attackers *apprehended*?

   (a)   20
   (b)   2
   (c)   10
   (d)   7

11.   Current research indicates that certain characteristics predispose a child to being abused. Which of the following is *not* such a factor?

   (a)   a child being born to unmarried parents
   (b)   children being born prematurely
   (c)   children born to large families
   (d)   children whose parents are substance abusers
   (e)   all of the above are such factors

12. In ____ *percent* of the cases of *child abuse* the abuser is a member of the child's immediate family.

    (a)   90
    (b)   75
    (c)   60
    (d)   50

13. Recent national data suggests that _____ *percent* of American children are victims of sexual assault by a parent or parent figure.

    (a)   1- 2
    (b)   5- 8
    (c)   10-20
    (d)   3- 4
    (e)   26-32

14. Approximately _____ elderly persons are victimized by physical abuse each year in the United States:

    (a)   100,000
    (b)   250,000
    (c)   550,000
    (d)   1.4 million
    (e)   10 million

Matching

a.	1883	g.	63
b.	infanticide	h.	1977
c.	one to four million	i.	force-only, obsessive, battering
d.	95	j.	39
e.	battered-woman syndrome	k.	4
f.	victim blaming	l.	long-term effects of child abuse

1. The estimated number of children between the ages of 3-17 who are abused by parents, grandparents, or guardians each year. _C_

2. Essentially, justifying the unequal treatment of an individual or group by finding defects in the victims rather than by examining the social and economic factors that contribute to their condition. _F_

3. The year in which the first state in the U.S. repealed the marital exemption clause to the rape statute. _h_

4. The year in which wife beating was banned in the United States. _a_

5. Percentage of abused children who are under the age of six. _j_

6. Percentage of all spousal or partner assaults that are committed by men. _d_

7. Estimated percentage of the elderly who are abused each year. _k_

8. The killing of infants and young children. _b_
9. Emotional problems, behavioral problems, cognitive problems, and physical ailments. _l_
10. Types of marital rape. _i_
11. Defined in terms of frequency, severity, intent to harm, and the ability to demonstrate injury. _e_
12. The percentage of rapes committed by husbands or acquaintances. _g_

Fill-In

1. Not until _1883_ was *wife beating* banned in the United States.
2. The *types of family violence* identified in the text include violence against _women_, violence against _children_, violence against the _elderly_, and violence against _siblings_.
3. _infanticide_ refers to the killing of infants and young children.
4. Four common *myths about family violence* include: family violence is _rare_, only _mentally ill_ people abuse family members, family violence is essentially a problem of the _lower class_, and _love_ is absent in violent families.
5. _95_ *percent* of all spousal or partner assaults are committed by *men*.
6. In general, the pattern of the battering experienced by women is referred to as the _battered - women syndrome_.
7. Four *explanations* of why spousal or partner abuse is so common in our society includes social _stress_, _power_, _dependency_, and _alcohol_.
8. Six important variables associated with violence in intimate relationships include: a high level of family or intimate _conflict_, a high level of _societal_ violence, family _socialization_ in violence, cultural norms that _legitimate_ family or intimate violence, _gender_ stereotypic socialization and sexual inequality, and the _privacy_ of the American family.
9. Common reasons why women *stay in violent relationships* include _children_, economic _dependence_, _religious_ beliefs, _fear_ of being alone, and _love_.
10. Two of the most persistent *rape myths* are that male sexual violence is caused by the attitudes and behaviors of _the victim_, and _African Americans_ are the primary perpetrators of rape.
11. In 1977, _Oregon_ became the first state to repeal the marital exemption clause to its *rape statute*. Since then, similar clauses have been eliminated or modified in about _5_ the states.
12. Three *types of marital rape* are identified in the text, including _force-only_ rape, _obsessive_ rape, and _battering_ rape.
13. _50_ *percent* of all *convicted rapists* are sentenced to less than one year in prison, with _25_ *percent* being sentenced to no jail time at all.
14. The harm men inflict on women takes many forms and has a wide range of effect. While the physical effects are most obvious, there is a tremendous toll exacted psychologically, emotionally, and financially. Research has found, for example, that during and after battering, woman tend to think very _poorly_ of themselves.
15. *Coping strategies* used by battered women include _psychological_ and _emotional_, self-_destructive_, _fighting-back_.
16. Battered women account for _42_ *percent* of all suicide attempts.
17. It is estimated that as many as _one-third_ of all *abuse and neglect cases* against children go unreported or undetected, especially if they involve _middle-class_ or _wealthy_ families.

18. An examination of the age of child abuse and neglect victims shows _____ *percent* are under the age of six, _____ *percent* are six to thirteen years of age, and _____ *percent* are between the ages of fourteen and seventeen.

19. Most *elder abuse* is perpetrated by _male adults_ (58 percent), followed by _children_ (28 percent).

20. *Sibling violence* is higher among children in families in which _child_ and _spouse_ assault also occur.

Short-Answer

1. What are some examples of folkways and mores in cultures around the world showing the *universality of violence against women*?

2. What are the historical indicators of how socially acceptable violence against *children* has been in our society?

3. What are some of the demographic facts that indicate the family is a *violent social institution* in our society?

4. Why do battered women *stay in battering relationships*?

5. What are the major factors associated with *spousal abuse*?

6. What are the important signs that suggest a woman might be in an *abusive relationship*?

7. What are the different *coping strategies* of women in abusive relationships? Describe each of these.

8. What are five *myths about rape*?

9. What is meant by the *rape syndrome*? What are the cultural conditions that create and maintain this pattern in society?

10. What is the evidence that the *criminal justice system* discriminates against women in cases of sexual assault?

11. What is the *prevalence of child abuse* in our society? What are the major factors associated with this social problem?

12. How prevalent is *child sexual abuse*? What children are at greatest risk? Who are the most likely perpetrators?

PART VI: ANSWERS TO STUDY QUESTIONS

True-False

1.	T	(p. 320)	9.	F	(p. 337)
2.	F	(p. 320)	10.	T	(p. 340)
3.	T	(p. 323)	11.	F	(p. 343)
4.	T	(p. 324)	12.	F	(p. 345)
5.	T	(p. 330)	13.	T	(p. 346)
6.	T	(p. 333)	14.	F	(p. 349)
7.	T	(p. 334)	15.	T	(p. 350)
8.	T	(p. 334)			

Multiple-Choice

1.	b	(p. 320)	8.	c	(p. 329)
2.	a	(p. 320)	9.	d	(p. 336)
3.	d	(p. 322)	10.	b	(p. 338)
4.	c	(p. 323)	11.	e	(p. 345)
5.	a	(p. 325)	12.	a	(p. 346)
6.	b	(p. 326)	13.	c	(p. 347)
7.	d	(p. 328)	14.	d	(p. 348)

Matching

1.	c	(p. 325)	7.	k	(p. 348)
2.	f	(p. 331)	8.	b	(p. 321)
3.	h	(p. 336)	9.	l	(p. 348)
4.	a	(p. 320)	10.	i	(p. 336)
5.	j	(p. 345)	11.	e	(p. 328)
6.	d	(p. 327)	12.	g	(p. 334)

Fill-In

1. 1883 (p. 320)
2. women, children, elderly, sibling (pp. 320-322)
3. Infanticide (p. 321)
4. rare, mentally ill, lower classes, love (pp. 325-327)
5. 95 (p. 327)
6. battered woman syndrome (p. 328)
7. stress, power, dependency, alcohol (p. 330)
8. conflict, societal, socialization, legitimate, gender, privacy (p. 331)
9. fear, dependence, children, love (pp. 332-333)
10. female victims, African American males (p. 335)
11. Oregon, one-half (p. 336)
12. force-only, battering, obsessive (p. 336)
13. 50, 25 (p. 338)
14. poorly (p. 339)
15. psychological, emotional, destructive, fighting back (pp. 339-340)
16. 42 (p. 340)
17. one-third, middle-class, wealthy (p. 345)
18. 39, 43, 15 (p. 345)
19. male adults, children (p. 349)
20. child, spouse (p. 350)

PART VII: IN FOCUS--IMPORTANT ISSUES

- The Roots of Family Violence: A Historical Context

  Identify and comment on three *historical facts* listed in the text concerning violence against women.

  Four *types of family violence* are identified in the text, including:

- Family Violence and U.S. Culture

  Identify four demographic patterns concerning the *nature and scope* of domestic violence:

- Myths About Violence and Abuse

  What are the four *myths* about family violence identified by the authors? Provide one piece of evidence for each which supports the authors' argument that these are myths.

- Physical Assault: The Case of Battered Women

  Identify three facts concerning the *prevalence of woman battering*:

  Four *theories of spousal or partner abuse* are:

  What are six important variables associated with *violence in intimate relationships*:

  What are four major reasons why women stay in *abusive relationships*?

- The Sexual Assault of Women

    What are five major *rape myths* identified in the text?

    What are three major points being made by the authors about *marital rape*?

- The Criminal Justice Response to Woman Assault

    What are two patterns identified by the authors to suggest that women are discriminated against in the criminal justice system when it comes to *violent crime*?

- The Effects of Physical and Sexual Assault on Women

    Identify and describe the three major *coping strategies* used by women in abusive relationships:

- A Comparative Look at Battered Men

    What is the evidence concerning *female violence against males*?

- Child Assault and Abuse

    What characteristics of children themselves put them at risk of *child abuse and neglect*?

    Who are most likely to be the *abusers of children*?

- Elder Abuse in the United States

  How is *elder abuse* defined?

  How prevalent is elder abuse?

- Sibling Abuse

  What factors seem to be more closely associated with *sibling abuse*?

PART VIII: ANALYSIS AND COMMENT

- In Other Places: "Rape, Italian Style" (p. 337)

  Key Points: Questions/Comments:

- Family Profile: "Laura Anderson" (p. 341)

  Key Points: Questions/Comments:

- Writing Your Own Script: "Recognizing Abusive Behavior" (p. 350)

  Key Points: Questions/Comments:

12 The Process of Uncoupling: Divorce in the United States

PART I: CHAPTER OUTINE

PART II: LEARNING OBJECTIVES

1.   To trace the demographic patterns of divorce in the U.S. from colonial times to the present.
2.   To describe the factors that affect marital stability.
3.   To identify the stages of divorce.
4.   To describe no-fault divorce and the effects it has on women.
5.   To discuss the influence on divorce of race, ethnicity, and socioeconomic status.
6.   To discuss the problems which family therapists believe are the most damaging to couple relationships, and also those problems that are believed to be the most difficult to treat.
7.   To describe the consequences of divorce on both women and men.
8.   To describe and differentiate between the short-term and long-term effects of divorce on children.
9.   To describe the changing patterns of child custody.
10.   To describe other ways, besides divorce, in which marriage may be disrupted.

PART III: KEY TERMS

alimony

annulment

community divorce

conciliation counseling

coparent divorce

desertion

divorce

divorce counseling

divorce mediation

divorce rate

economic divorce

emotional divorce

legal divorce

no-fault divorce

joint custody

psychic divorce

separation

sole custody

split custody

stations of divorce

PART IV: IMPORTANT RESEARCHERS

Constance Ahrons and George Levinger

Jessie Bernard

Paul Bohannan

Cheryl Buehler and Mary Langenbrumer

Frank Furstenberg and Andrew Cherlin

William Galston

James Ponzetti and Rodney Cate

Paul Rasmussen and Kathleen Ferraro

Glenda Riley

Judith Wallerstein

Judith Wallerstein and Sandra Blakeslee

PART V: STUDY QUESTIONS

True-False

1. *Desertion* was the most common ground for women obtaining a divorce during the nineteenth century in the United States. T (F)
2. *Divorce rates* among the Hopi has historically been extremely low relative to other cultures. T (F)
3. Divorce rates among *Latinas/os* are higher than other racial and ethnic groups in the United States today. T (F)
4. Overall, the lower the income level, the *higher* the divorce rate. (T) F
5. Marital disruption is more likely when the marriage is *child-free*. T (F)
6. People whose parents divorced have *lower divorce rates* than do children who come from intact families. T (F)
7. Social Science research has found divorce to be a *process*, involving several stages that both spouses go through. (T) F
8. *Women* appear to take a more active role in preparing and planning for divorce and separation than do men. T (F)
9. Family therapists claim that two of the easiest *areas of problems in a marriage* to treat are power struggles and unrealistic expectations of marriage or spouse. T (F)
10. Research suggests that divorced people are almost *equally likely* to report both positive and negative outcomes. T F
11. Despite their economic stress, evidence suggests that women fare better than men in terms of *divorce adjustment*. (T) F   TRUE
12. Research suggests younger women (under forty years of age) fared better in terms of *making life changes* than did men or older women. T (F)
13. Women tend to *remarry* sooner after a divorce than men. T (F)
14. Over sixty percent of *African American* children live in single-parent families. T (F)
15. Less than one-quarter of children from divorced families go to *college*. T (F)
16. *Joint custody* can take two forms, including *legal* and *physical*. T (F)
17. According to the authors, d*ivorce mediation* is defined as the process of helping people conclude the psychic divorce process. T F
18. Under *no-fault divorce*, a divorce is granted even if only one spouse wants it. T (F)
19. *Separation* refers to the termination of marital cohabitation and can take a variety of forms. (T) F
20. A civil *annulment* legally states that the marriage never existed. (T) F

Multiple-Choice

1. Approximately _____ married couples *divorce* each year in the United States.

   (a)   200,000
   (b)   750,000
   (c)   1,200,000
   (d)   500,000
   (e)   2,100,000

2. According to historian *Glenda Riley*, social and economic reasons for divorce during colonial times included:

   (a) growing mobility of colonists.
   (b) emergence of a market economy.
   (c) movement west.
   (d) new technologies.
   (e) all of the above.

3. Which of the following statements concerning a cross-cultural perspective on divorce *not accurate*?

   (a) Among the matrilineal Hopi clan women and men could both initiate a divorce, and divorce has traditionally been easy to get.
   (b) In traditional Chinese society, only men could initiate a divorce.
   (c) In Taiwan the divorce rate has significantly increased over the past twenty years.
   (d) In Taiwan, women are favored in the courts when it comes to property and children.

4. Which was the first state to recognize *no-fault divorce*?

   (a) New York
   (b) California
   (c) Nevada
   (d) Maine
   (e) Florida

5. Which of the following groups has the *lowest divorce rate*?

   (a) Latina/os
   (b) African Americans
   (c) whites
   (d) Native Americans

6. A number of factors identified as being associated with *divorce* have been found by family researchers, including:

   (a) education and religion.
   (b) parental divorce.
   (c) presence of children.
   (d) income.
   (e) all of the above.

7. Couples of which of the following *religious groups* has the lowest divorce rate?

   (a) Catholics
   (b) Protestants
   (c) Jews
   (d) all three groups have equivalent divorce rates

160

8. *Paul Bohannan* has identified *six divorces experienced* by couples during dissolution of a marriage which he called the:

   (a) dissolution process.
   (b) stations of divorce.
   (c) cost-and-benefits considerations.
   (d) the uncoupling continuum.

9. Which of the following is *not* identified as one of the divorces in *Paul Bohannan's* schema?

   (a) emotional divorce
   (b) economic divorce
   (c) psychic divorce
   (d) social divorce

10. The *American Association of Marriage and Family Therapists* rated _____ as the most damaging aspect of couple relationships.

   (a) power struggles
   (b) lack of loving feelings
   (c) lack of demonstration of affection
   (d) communication problems

11. According to research in which divorced people are given a list of experiences to choose from, the *most frequently* selected one was:

   (a) I have felt insecure.
   (b) I have felt angry toward my former spouse.
   (c) I have felt worthwhile as a person.
   (d) I have been depressed.

12. The *American Association of Marriage and Family Therapists* considered the problem of _____ in marriage to be the *most difficult to treat.*

   (a) alcoholism
   (b) lack of loving feelings
   (c) power struggles
   (d) value conflicts

13. The most striking difference between *women* and *men* following a divorce is a _____ one.

   (a) emotional
   (b) psychological
   (c) social
   (d) physical
   (e) monetary

14. Currently, the courts award *alimony* in approximately _____ *percent* of divorce cases.

    (a)   5
    (b)   15
    (c)   40
    (d)   55
    (e)   25

15. What percentage of children under the age of eighteen live in *single-parent families* today?

    (a)   14
    (b)   24
    (c)   32
    (d)   45
    (e)   51

16. What is the procedure designed to *help divorcing couples negotiate* a fair and mutually agreed-upon resolution to their problems?

    (a)   conciliation counseling
    (b)   divorce counseling
    (c)   articulation counseling
    (d)   divorce mediation

Matching

a.	alimony	f.	conciliation counseling
b.	stations of divorce	g.	divorce mediation
c.	psychic divorce	h.	separation
d.	joint custody	i.	desertion
e.	divorce counseling	j.	annulment

1. Efforts aimed at helping people conclude the psychic divorce. _e_
2. Involves a redefinition of self away from the mutuality of couplehood and back to a sense of singlehood. _c_
3. A procedure designed to help divorcing couples negotiate a fair and mutually agreed-upon resolution of such issues as marital property distribution, child custody, visitation rights, and financial support. _g_
4. Emotional, legal, economic, coparental, community, psychic. _b_
5. Refers to the termination of marital cohabitation and can take many forms. _h_
6. Legally states that the marriage never existed and, thus the parties are free to marry at will. _j_
7. Its purpose is to see whether the marital problems can be resolved and the couple reconciled. _f_
8. A concept originating in England in the 1650s, whereby a husband deemed to be at fault for the dissolution of the marriage was required to provide his wife with a financial allowance. _a_
9. Refers to the abandonment of a spouse or family. _i_
10. Means both parents are involved in child-rearing and decision-making. _d_

Fill-In

1. Divorce has been a part of U.S. history since _____ when a *Puritan court* in Massachusetts granted the first divorce decree in colonial America.
2. The *divorce rate* refers to the number of *divorces* occurring annually for every 1000 people.
3. The *divorce rate* reached an all-time high in the U.S. in _____ and has been declining ever since.
4. Two factors are often cited to explain the relatively high level of *marital stability among Latinas/os* are *cultural traditions* and *religion*.
5. Important factors affecting *martial stability* in the U.S. include *age* at first marriage, *religion*, *education*, *income*, and parental *divorce* and presence of *children*.
6. The majority of separations and divorces follow a period of personal unhappiness, conflict, and deliberation, during which time individuals make decisions based upon three types of criteria (a) an evaluation of the *attractiveness* of the relationship itself, (b) and evaluation of the *cost* and *benefits* of a divorce and (c) an evaluation of the *attractiveness* of possible alternatives.
7. Anthropologist *Paul Bohannan* has identified not one but six divorces that couples experience in dissolving their marital relationship. He called these the *stations of divorce* and includes _____, _____, _____, _____, _____, and _____.
8. Two key factors affecting the *divorce rate* over the last generation includes changes in *attitudes* and changes in the *economy*.
9. The behaviors cited by divorced people as leading to *divorce* include poor *communication*, *extramarital* sex, constant *fighting*, *drug* abuse, *alcohol* or _____ abuse, _____ or _____ problems, and *financial* mismanagement.
10. According to researcher *Jessie Bernard*, the most striking difference between women and men following a divorce is a _____ one.
11. Newly dating divorced people must deal with *two key issues*: how to explain their _____ *status* and whether to be _____ *active*.
12. Two key factors explain the *downward social mobility* of women and their children after a divorce: the _____ gap between women and men, and the failure of _____ to award, and the ex-husbands to pay _____ and _____.
13. *Joint custody* can take two forms: joint _____ custody, in which both parents share decision making on such issues as education aand health care, and joint _____ custody, which covers how much time children will spend living with each parent.
14. _____ refers to the termination of marital cohabitation and can take a variety of forms.
15. _____ legally states that the marriage never existed and, thus the parties are free to marry at will.

Short-Answer

1.   Differentiate between *his* and *her* divorces.
2.   What are the general patterns concerning the *short-term* and *long-term* effects of divorce on children.
3.   What does the research show about the *negative consequences* of divorce on husbands and wives?
4.   What are the *stages of divorce*? Describe each. How are these stages experienced differently by husbands and wives?
5.   What are the areas of marriage most damaging for couples experiencing marital difficulties?
6.   What are the major *societal factors* affecting divorce rates in our society?
7.   What are the general *demographic patterns of divorce* in our society? That is, what characteristics of a person puts he or she at risk of divorce?
8.   What factors do *divorced people* most commonly cite as leading them to divorce?
9.   What factors do *family therapists* see as the most difficult to work with among couples with marital difficulties?
10. What does the data show concerning men and women *recovering* from divorce?

PART VI: ANSWERS TO STUDY QUESTIONS

True-False

1.	T	(p. 355)	11.	T	(p. 370)
2.	F	(p. 356)	12.	T	(p. 371)
3.	F	(p. 357)	13.	F	(p. 371)
4.	T	(p. 359)	14.	T	(p. 372)
5.	T	(p. 360)	15.	F	(p. 373)
6.	F	(p. 360)	16.	T	(p. 374)
7.	T	(p, 361)	17.	F	(p. 376)
8.	T	(p. 362)	18.	T	(p. 377)
9.	F	(p. 365)	19.	T	(p. 378)
10.	T	(p. 365)	20.	T	(p. 379)

Multiple-Choice

1.	c	(p. 354)	9.	d	(pp. 362-363)
2.	e	(p. 355)	10.	d	(p. 365)
3.	d	(p. 355)	11.	c	(p. 365)
4.	b	(pp. 356-357)	12.	a	(p. 365)
5.	a	(p. 357)	13.	e	(p. 367)
6.	e	(pp. 359-360)	14.	b	(p. 368)
7.	c	(p. 360)	15.	c	(p. 372)
8.	b	(p. 362)	16.	d	(pp. 376-377)

Matching

1.	e	(p. 376)	6.	j	(p. 379)
2.	c	(p. 363)	7.	f	(p. 376)
3.	g	(pp. 376-377)	8.	a	(p. 354)
4.	b	(p. 362)	9.	i	(p. 378)
5.	h	(p. 378)	10.	d	(p. 374)

Fill-In

1. 1639 (p. 354)
2. divorce rate (p. 357)
3. 1980 (p. 357)
4. cultural traditions, religion (p. 358)
5. age, education, income, religion, divorce, children (pp. 359-360)
6. attractiveness, costs, benefits, attractiveness (p. 361)
7. emotional, legal, economic, coparental, community, psychic (p. 363)
8. attitudes, economy (p. 364)
9. communication, extramarital, fighting, drug, alcohol, financial (p. 364)
10. monetary (p. 367)
11. unmarried, sexually (p. 367)
12. earnings, courts, alimony, child support (p. 368)
13. legal, physical (p. 374)
14. Separation (p. 378)
15. Annulment (p. 379)

PART VII: IN FOCUS--IMPORTANT ISSUES

- Historical Perspectives

What social factors affected the divorce rate in *colonial America*?

What were the findings of a 1887 Congressional study on divorce?

How did *World War I* and *World War II* affect the divorce rate in the United States?

Briefly describe divorce rate patterns for the following *racial* and *ethnic groups*:

African Americans

Latiinas/os

165

- Who Gets Divorced and Why?

    How are each of the following factors related to divorce rates?

    Age at first marriage:

    Education:

    Income:

    Religion:

    Parental divorce:

    Presence of children:

- The Process of Divorce

    What are the *stages* in the divorce process?

    Define each of the following *stations of divorce*:

    Emotional:

    Legal:

    Economic:

    Coparental:

    Community:

    Psychic:

- Causes of Divorce

    What are the two major factors identified as influencing the divorce rate over the last one or two generations? Provide two *illustrations* for each of these.

    From the perspective of *divorced people*, what are the main reasons for getting a divorce?

    What areas are identified by *family therapists* as being damaging to a marriage?

- The Impact of Divorce on Spouses

    What are the most common *consequences of divorce*? How are these different for women and men?

    Describe *"his" divorce*:

    Describe *"her" divorce*:

    How do women and men *recover from divorce* differently?

- The Impact of Divorce on Children

    What are the *short-term effects* of divorce on children?

    What are the *long-term effects* of divorce on children?

167

Identify and define the major types of *child custody*:

*   Reaching Accord: Divorce Counseling and Mediation

    Differentiate between *divorce counseling, conciliation counseling,* and *divorce mediation.*

*   The Divorce Debate Revisited

    What are the *reforms* currently being debated and/or enacted in our society regarding divorce?

PART VIII: ANALYSIS AND COMMENT

*   In Other Places: "Cross-Cultural Patterns in Divorce" (p. 356)

    Key Points: Questions/Comments:

*   Applying the Sociological Imagination: "Are You at Risk?" (p. 361)

    Key Points: Questions/Comments:

- Strengthening Marriages and Families: "Resolving Problems" (p. 366)

    Key Points: Questions/Comments:

- Social Policy Issues: "Who Receives Child Support" (p. 369)

    Key Points: Questions/Comments:

- Searching the Internet: "Children's Rights in Regard to Custody and Visitation" (p. 375)

    Key Points: Questions/Comments:

- Writing Your Own Script: "Evaluating Relationships" (p. 377)

    Key Points: Questions/Comments:

169

13 Remarriage and Remarried Families

PART I: CHAPTER OUTLINE

I.   Historical Perspective
II.   Cultural Images of Stepfamilies
III.   The Process of Remarriage
       A.   Dating and Courtship Patterns
       B.   The Decision to Remarry
       C.   Patterns of Remarriage
       D.   The Stations of Remarriage
IV.   Stages in the Development of Remarried Families
V.   Remarried Families: Roles, Interactions, and Reactions
       A.   Children and the Remarriage Service
       B.   Children in Remarried Families
       C.   Stepmothers: A Bad Rap?
       D.   Stepfathers: Polite Strangers?
       E.   Ex-Spouses: Do They Fade Away?
VI.   The Strengths and Benefits of Remarried Families
VII.   The Quality of the Remarital Relationship
       A.   Stability in Remarriage
VIII.   Recommendations for Social Policy
       A.   Clarification of Legal Norms
       B.   Modification of the Tax Code
       C.   Education
IX.   Summary
X.   Key Terms
XI.   Questions for Study and Reflection
XII.   Further Reading

PART II: LEARNING OBJECTIVES

1.   To describe the concept of remarriage from an historical perspective.
2.   To identify and discuss the social factors influencing the decision to remarry.
3.   To describe the patterns of remarriage in terms of social class, race, ethnicity, education and presence of children.
4.   To identify and describe the five stations of remarriage.

170

5. To provide an overview of the typical reactions to and consequences of parental remarriage for children.
6. To identify and discuss factors that affect stability in remarriages.
7. To identify and discuss the positive aspects of remarried families.
8. To identify and discuss three policy recommendations concerning remarried families in our society.

PART III: KEY TERMS

community remarriage

emotional remarriage

legal remarriage

overlapping households

parental remarriage

psychic remarriage

remarried family

PART IV: IMPORTANT RESEARCHERS

William Beer

Margaret Draughon

Elizabeth Einstein

Barbara Fishman

Frank Furstenberg and Graham Spanier

Ann Goetting

Penny Gross

Lynn White and Agnes Riedman

PART V: STUDY QUESTIONS

True-False

1. A recently published longitudinal study on *remarriages* found the remarriage is easiest when children are very young and toughest when kids are ages 10-14. (T) F
2. The United States has the highest *remarriage rate* in the world. T F
3. In America during the seventeenth and eighteenth centuries the *remarriage rate* was approximately twenty to thirty percent. (T) F
4. Remarriages today in the United States are actually more likely than was true in past generations to follow a *death* rather than a divorce. T (F)
5. Research has found that older adults report many of the same anxieties about *dating* that adolescents report. (T) F
6. Divorced people *remarry* at a much higher rate than do widowed people. T (F)
7. Studies show that more than one-half of all women who divorce *in their 40s and 50s* eventually remarry. (T) F
8. Compared to most other categories, *lower-class African Americans* are more likely to remarry after a divorce. T (F)
9. Divorced men with children are *more like to remarry sooner* than their female counterparts. (T) F
10. *Rates of remarriage*, while varying by age, do not vary very much across social class, race, or ethnicity. T (F)
11. Among remarried families compared to *romantic families* and *matriarchal families*, *neotraditional families* tend to be the most successful. (T) F
12. Studies suggest that if parent remarriage occurs *early* in a child's life, the child experiences few adverse effects. (T) F
13. Social Science research has consistently shown that *girls* have more problems adjusting to divorce than boys. T (F)
14. The most common structure in *remarried families* in the United States is a biological mother, her children, and a stepfather. (T) F
15. In both first and remarriages men report *higher levels of satisfaction* than women. T F
16. Studies have found the the *divorce rate* is lower in remarriages with stepchildren. T (F)

Multiple-Choice

1. Approximately what percentage of marriages in the United States today involve a *second marriage* for at least one of the partners?

    (a)   3
    (b)   15
    (c)   30
    (d)   40
    (e)   65

172

2.   In which of the following ways, according to *William Beer*, does the *remarried family* differ from the nuclear family?

      (a)   lack of kinship terms
      (b)   complexity
      (c)   guilt
      (d)   grieving
      (e)   all of the above

3.   In colonial America, *marriages* were likely to last _____ years.

      (a)   3
      (b)   7
      (c)   16
      (d)   23
      (e)   42

4.   Which of the following terms is *preferred by our authors* to describe *stepfamilies*?

      (a)   remarried families
      (b)   blended families
      (c)   binuclear families
      (d)   merged families
      (e)   aggregate families

5.   Which of the following statements is *inaccurate* about *stepfamilies* in the United States?

      (a)   About sixty-five percent of remarriages involve children from a prior marriage.
      (b)   Sixty-five percent of children living with a stepparent live with a stepfather.
      (c)   About fifteen percent of all children in married-couple families are stepchildren.
      (d)   African American children are less likely to live in stepfamilies than are white children.

6.   Given the pain and trauma surrounding many divorces, and given the complications of resumed dating, why do so many Americans choose to *remarry*?

      (a)   Marriage remains an important cultural value.
      (b)   Reasons for remarriage are similar to reasons for first marriage--convenience, companionship, love.
      (c)   Remarriage may be a rational choice for many women who experience downward social mobility after a divorce.
      (d)   Divorced and widowed custodial parents may be motivated to remarry so they will have help raising their children.
      (e)   All of the above.

7. In the United States, less than _____ *percent* of women 40 years of age or older remarry.

   (a)   25
   (b)   4
   (c)   15
   (d)   55

8. The _____ *remarriage* generally receives the most attention in Social Science literature.

   (a)   emotional
   (b)   economic
   (c)   parental
   (d)   psychic

9. The _____ *remarriage* refers to the process of reestablishing a bond of attraction, love, commitment, and trust with another person.

   (a)   community
   (b)   emotional
   (c)   psychic
   (d)   cognitive

10. *Barbara Fishman* found that a(n) _____ *approach* to family finances is the most likely to unify a stepfamily.

   (a)   "two-pot"
   (b)   economic
   (c)   "common pot"
   (d)   legal

11. Which of the following patterns emerged *least frequently* in *Penny Gross's* study on children and parent-child relationships in remarried families?

   (a)   retention
   (b)   augmentation
   (c)   reduction
   (d)   substitution

12. Which of the following is *inaccurate* regarding the *consequences of parental remarriage for children*?

   (a)   In stepfamilies, girls experience more adjustment problems and report more adjustment problems and report poorer relationships with parents than do boys.
   (b)   Compared with stepdaughters, stepsons are more sullen, withdrawn, and direct more negative problem-solving behavior toward stepfathers.
   (c)   Girls in stepfamily households leave home to marry or live independently at an earlier age than those in single- or two-parent households.
   (d)   Boys are initially angry that dad was "sent away," but then they become comfortable with another male presence in the household.

174

13. Which of the following was *not* one of the themes in the research on *stepfamilies* conducted by *William Beers*?

    (a)   the role of half siblings
    (b)   stepsibling rivalry
    (c)   changes in age order
    (d)   stepsibling sexuality
    (e)   all are themes in this research

14. Approximately _____ *percent* of women are likely to have a child after remarrying.

    (a)   40
    (b)   20
    (c)   70
    (d)   50

15. *Margaret Draughon* suggested all of the following *except* _____ as possible relationships between *stepmothers* and *stepchildren*.

    (a)   primary mother
    (b)   friend
    (c)   counselor
    (d)   other mother

16. Which of the following was *not* one of the areas of difficulty between *stepfathers* and *stepchildren* as outlined by *Elizabeth Einstein*?

    (a)   rivalry for the mother's attention
    (b)   money
    (c)   discipline
    (d)   sex

17. Regarding the *quality of the remarital relationship* research has found which of the following?

    (a)   Successful stepfamilies require partners who not only can cope with the usual stresses of stepfamily living but who can successfully relinquish traditional gendered parental roles.
    (b)   Satisfaction seems to be higher in mother-stepfather families where the stepfather had children from a previous marriage than in stepfamilies where the stepfather coparented children from a previous marriage.
    (c)   Divorce rates are lower in remarriages with stepchildren.
    (d)   Divorce rates among remarried couples are significantly lower than divorce rates for first-time married couples.
    (e)   All of the above are accurate statements concerning what research has found about the quality of the remarital relationship.

18.   Which of the following is *not a recommendation* for social policy concerning remarried families?

(a)   clarification of legal norms
(b)   modification of the tax code
(c)   development of educational materials
(d)   all of the above are recommendations

Matching

a.	40	f.	psychic marriage
b.	remarried family	g.	neotraditional family
c.	65	h.	romantic family
d.	15	i.	policy recommendations
e.	emotional remarriage	j.	50

1.   Percentage of remarriages involving children from a prior marriage. _c_
2.   A two parent, two-generation unit that comes into being on the legal remarriage of a widowed or divorced person who has biological or adopted children from a prior union with whom he or she is regularly involved. _b_
3.   Tends to be the most successful type of remarriage. _g_
4.   The process of reestablishing a bond of attraction, love, commitment, and trust with another person. _e_
5.   Clarification of legal norms, modification of the tax code, and development of education materials. _i_
6.   The percentage of recent marriages in the U.S. involving a second marriage for at least one of the partners. _a_
7.   Percentage of first and remarriages that end in divorce. _j_
8.   Percentage of all children in married-couple families who are stepchildren. _d_
9.   Requires moving back from the recently acquired identity of single person to a couple identity. _f_
10.   Tends to be the least successful type of remarriage. _h_

Fill-In

1.   In the U.S. over __40__ *percent* of recent marriages involved a second marriage for at least one of the partners.
2.   During the seventeenth and eighteenth centuries the proportion of *remarriages* among all marriages was approximately __20__ to __30__ *percent*.
3.   Whereas, in early America the overwhelming majority of remarriages followed the __death__ of a spouse, today remarriages typically involve __divorced__ individuals.
4.   In early American colonial times the marriages lasted an average of __7__ years, and had a __33__ chance of lasting ten years.
5.   *Divorced* and *widowed* individuals who remarry tend to spend __half__ the time on dating and courtship that they did preceding their first marriage.
6.   For both women and men __social class__ may be more important than *age* in the decision to remarry.
7.   *Ann Goetting* found that there is a similarity between the developmental tasks that must be mastered in the __divorce__ *process* and many personal changes and adjustments that accompany the process of __remarriage__.

8. Remarriages in which one or both spouses have children from a previous relationship is known as a _parental_ remarriage.

9. Utilizing a structured interview technique that focused on parent-child relationships, researcher *Penny Gross* asked children who they considered to be family members. Four patterns emerged, including _retention_, _substitution_, _reduction_, and _augmentation_.

10. Roughly _half_ of all women who *remarry* will bear a child with their spouses.

11. *Margaret Draughon* suggests three possibilities for *stepmother roles*, including _other_, _primary_, and _friend_.

12. *Elizabeth Einstein* identified three *areas of difficulties for stepfathers*, including _sex_, _money_, and _discipline_.

13. Most recent research reinforces the view that successful stepfamilies require partners who not only can cope with the usual stresses of stepfamily living but who can successfully relinquish traditional _gendered_ parental roles.

14. The *recommendations for social policy* change concerning remarriages presented in the text include clarification of _legal norms_, modification of the _tax code_, and _education_.

Short-Answer

1. Briefly recount the *history of remarriage* from early colonial times in America to today.
2. What are the generalizations being made about the *characteristics of divorced people* in dating and courtship relationships?
3. How do *remarriage rates* vary by such variables as *age, race, ethnicity, social class*, and *education*.
4. What are the ways in which remarriages may be *stronger* than first marriages?
5. Identify five consequences of parental remarriage for *children*.
6. What are the issues raised in the text concerning the status of *stepfathers*.
7. What does the research suggest about *stability* in remarriages as compared to first marriages?
8. What are five tasks that confront stepfamilies? How are these different and similar for people in first and remarriages?

PART VI: ANSWERS TO STUDY QUESTIONS

True-False

1.	T	(p. 381)	9.	T	(p. 387)
2.	T	(p. 382)	10.	F	(p. 387)
3.	T	(p. 383)	11.	T	(p. 389)
4.	F	(p. 383)	12.	T	(p. 392)
5.	T	(p. 384)	13.	F	(p. 392)
6.	T	(p. 386)	14.	T	(p. 392)
7.	F	(p. 387)	15.	T	(p. 398)
8.	F	(p. 387)	16.	F	(p. 400)

Multiple-Choice

1.	d	(p. 382)	10.	c	(p. 389)
2.	e	(p. 382)	11.	d	(p. 391)
3.	b	(p. 383)	12.	b	(p. 392)
4.	a	(p. 384)	13.	e	(p. 393)
5.	d	(p. 385)	14.	d	(p. 394)
6.	e	(p. 386)	15.	c	(p. 395)
7.	c	(p. 387)	16.	a	(p. 396)
8.	c	(p. 388)	17.	b	(pp. 398-400)
9.	b	(p. 388)	18.	d	(pp. 401-402)

Matching

1.	c	(p. 385)	6.	a	(p. 382)
2.	b	(p. 382)	7.	j	(p. 401)
3.	g	(p. 389)	8.	d	(p. 385)
4.	e	(p. 388)	9.	f	(p. 388)
5.	i	(pp. 401-402)	10.	h	(p. 389)

Fill-In

1. 40 (p. 382)
2. 20, 30 (p. 383)
3. death, divorced (p. 383)
4. 7, 33 (p. 383)
5. half (p. 385)
6. social class (p. 387)
7. divorce, remarriage (p. 388)
8. parental (p. 388)
9. retention, substitution, reduction, augmentation (p. 391)
10. half (p. 394)
11. other, primary, friend (p. 395)
12. sex, money, discipline (p. 396)
13. gendered (p. 398)
14. legal norms, tax code, education (pp. 401-402)

PART VII: IN FOCUS--IMPORTANT ISSUES

According to William Beer, what are the ten fundamental ways in which the *remarried family* is different from the nuclear family?

- Historical Perspective

  In comparison to colonial America, in what ways are *remarried families* similar today?

- Cultural Images of Stepfamilies

  Why do our authors prefer the term *remarried families* to describe stepfamilies?

- The Process of Remarriage

  What are four social factors that influence a person's decision to *remarry*?

  How do each of the following affect patterns of *remarriage*?

  Social Class and Education

  Social Class, Race and Ethnicity

  The Presence of Children

  Define each of the following *stations of remarriage*:

  economic

  emotional

  community

  parental

  economic

  legal

- Stages in the Development of Remarried Families

  Differentiate between the following *types of remarried families*:

  Neotraditional

  Romantic

  Matriarchal

  Describe each of the following patterns concerning *children's perceptions of family membership*:

  retention

  substitution

  reduction

  augmentation

- Remarried Families: Roles, Interactions, and Reactions

  How does the *sex* and *age* of a child affect how children experience a remarried family?

  How do our authors categorize and describe *stepmothers*?

  How do our authors categorize and describe *stepfathers*?

- The Strengths and Benefits of Remarried Families

  Identify four benefits or strengths of *remarried families*:

- The Quality of the Remarital Relationship

  How do each of the following affect *stability in remarriage*?

  Outside Support and Pressures

  The Presence of Children

  Time

- Recommendations for Social Policy

  Provide an example for each of the following *recommendations*:

  Clarification of Legal Norms

  Modification of the Tax Code

  Education

PART VIII: ANALYSIS AND COMMENT

- Searching the Internet: "Children in Stepfamilies" (p. 385)

  Key Points: Questions/Comments:

- Family Profile: "The Maring Family" (p. 398)

    Key Points: Questions/Comments:

- Applying the Sociological Imagination: "What's in a Card?" (p. 401)

    Key Points: Questions/Comments:

- Writing Your Own Script: "Thinking About Remarriage" (p. 402)

    Key Points: Questions/Comments:

14 | Families in Later Life

PART I: CHAPTER OUTLINE

I.   Characteristics of Later-Life Families
   A.   The Sandwich Generation
   B.   Diversity in the Family Life Cycle
   C.   Changing Age Norms
II.   The Demographics of Aging: Defining "Old"
   A.   Age Categories of the Elderly
   B.   Gender and Marital Status
   C.   Race, Ethnicity, and Class
   D.   Poverty among the Elderly
III.   Living Arrangements
   A.   Housing Patterns
IV.   Marriages In Later Life
   A.   Marital Quality and Satisfaction
   B.   Adjustment to Retirement
   C.   Intergenerational Relationships
   D.   Quality of Relationships
   E.   Patterns of Support
V.   Evolving Patterns of Kinship: Grandparenthood
   A.   Style of Grandparenting
   B.   Benefits and Conflicts
   C.   Great-Grandparenthood
VI.   The Child-Free Elderly
VII.   Sibling Relationships
VIII.   Health and Illness
   A.   The Spouse as Caregiver
   B.   Adult Children as Caregivers
IX.   The Experience of Widowhood
   A.   Stages of Widowhood
   B.   Gender Differences in Widowhood
   C.   Beyond Widowhood
X.   Implications for Social Policy
XI.   Summary
XII.   Key Terms
XIII.   Questions for Study and Reflection
XIV.   Further Reading

PART II: LEARNING OBJECTIVES

1. To describe the demographic and social characteristics of families in the later stages of the family life cycle.
2. To identify and describe the most widely recognized age categories of the elderly.
3. To discuss the myths and realities of housing patterns among the elderly.
4. To discuss the nature of marriage in late life with respect to the quality, satisfaction levels, and adjustment patterns of retirement.
5. To describe the essential characteristics of grandparenting in U.S. society today.
6. To describe the realities of health, illness, and caregiving with regard to the elderly in the United States today.
7. To discuss the experience of widowhood in U.S. society.

PART III: KEY TERMS

ageism

age norms

boomerang generation

functional age

sandwich generation

social gerontology

PART IV: IMPORTANT RESEARCHERS

Linda Ade-Ridder   Linda Ade-Ridder and Timothy Brubaker

Felix Berado   Timothy Brubaker

Robert DiGuilo   Vira Kivitt

Elisabeth Kubler-Ross   Gary Lee and Constance Shehan

Helen Lopata   Elizabeth Murran

Bernice Neugarten and Karol Weinstein   Erdman Palmore

Robert Rubinstein   Judith Treas

PART V: STUDY QUESTIONS

<u>True-False</u>

1. By the year 2050 it is expected that the *elderly* (people sixty-five years of age or older) will account for *twenty percent* of the U.S. population. T F
2. According to the U.S. Census Bureau, about *twelve percent* of young adults aged 25-34 live with their parents. T F
3. *Age norms* refer to an individual's physical, intellectual, and social capacities in relation to members of their age cohort or peers. T F
4. In the U.S. today there are about *four times* as many *widows* as *widowers*. T F
5. Most men over the age of sixty-five in the U.S. are *married*. T F
6. *Poverty rates* among the aged in the U.S. are higher today than in decades past. T F
7. The vast majority of older people maintain their independence in the community, living *alone or in a household with a spouse*. T F
8. *African American women and men* over the age of sixty-five are more likely to be living with relatives than their white counterparts. T F
9. Less than one-half of the elderly in the U.S. *own their homes*. T F
10. The elderly today in the United States are *less likely* to live in deficient housing than in generations past. T F

11. Recent studies have found that over the course of a marriage there is a *curvilinear relationship* between years married and marital quality and happiness.   T F
12. Most older people in the U.S. live over 100 miles from their adult children.   T F
13. Research indicates that there is more contact with *maternal grandparents* and that the maternal grandmother was consistently listed as the grandparent to whom grandchildren felt closest.   T F
14. Being *child-free* is a predictor of social isolation in later life.   T F
15. Upward of seventy to eighty percent of all elderly adults in the United States have at least one *living sibling*.   T F
16. Seventy percent of the noninstitutionalized elderly in the United States report their *health* as good or excellent.   T F
17. The *first stage* of *widowhood* for males is termed *emergence*.   T F
18. A larger percentage of white women over the age of sixty-five are *widowed* as compared to African American women.   T F

Multiple-Choice

1. Approximately _____ percent of the U.S. population today is over the age of *sixty-five*.

    (a)   5
    (b)   8
    (c)   13
    (d)   18
    (e)   23

2. According to *Timothy Brubaker, later-life families*:

    (a)   have lengthy family histories.
    (b)   are multigenerational.
    (c)   experience a number of new life events for which they have little preparation.
    (d)   all of the above.
    (e)   none of the above.

3. By the year 2050 the number of elderly Americans is expected to be approximately _____ *million*, or twenty percent of the total U.S. population.

    (a)   58
    (b)   80
    (c)   45
    (d)   98
    (e)   34

4. The *boomerang generation* refers to:

    (a)   the large percentage of young adults today moving back into the residence of their parents.

    (b)   older people remarrying after the death of a spouse and repeating earlier stages in the family life cycle.

    (c)   the tendency of relationships with kin, especially one's children to be "patched up" before the death of an aged relative.

    (d)   the pattern whereby each generation, as they age, begins to develop attitudes and behaviors similar to generations past.

5. During the decade of the 1990s, approximately _____ *percent* of unmarried adults aged 25-34 *lived with their parents*.

    (a)   12
    (b)   22
    (c)   32
    (d)   42
    (e)   6

6. What is the term used to describe the stereotypes and the discriminatory treatment of the *elderly*?

    (a)   gerontocracy
    (b)   social gerontology
    (c)   ageism
    (d)   none of the above

7. Which of the following is *not* one of the categories of older people currently recognized by gerontologists?

    (a)   old-old
    (b)   young-old
    (c)   newly-old
    (d)   middle-old

8. Approximately _____ *percent* of older Americans are *female*.

    (a)   45
    (b)   50
    (c)   55
    (d)   60
    (e)   75

9. Today in the United States, *eighty-four percent* of people over the age of sixty-five are white while
_____ *percent* are African American.

   (a)   40
   (b)   30
   (c)   20
   (d)   8
   (e)   2

10. The vast majority of *elderly people* in the U.S. live:

   (a)   in nursing homes.
   (b)   with members of their extended families.
   (c)   alone or with their spouse.
   (d)   none of the above.

11. At any given time, what percentage of the elderly in the U.S. live in *nursing homes*?

   (a)   5
   (b)   10
   (c)   15
   (d)   20
   (e)   25

12. According to research by *Linda Ade-Ridder* and *Timothy Brubaker, marital quality* _____ with age.

   (a)   improves
   (b)   remains the same
   (c)   declines
   (d)   there was no consensus on this question

13. Which of the following patterns of *retirement* among older couples was *not* identified by *Timothy
Brubaker*?

   (a)   dissynchronized-husband initially
   (b)   dissynchronized-wife initially
   (c)   dissynchronized-jointly
   (d)   single or traditional retirement

14. Which of the following situations has been found to produce the *least amount of marital satisfaction*
among older American wives?

   (a)   husband working, wife retired
   (b)   wife working, husband retired
   (c)   husband and wife both working
   (d)   husband and wife both retired

15. According to research by *Judith Treas*, most older people see their incomes:

    (a)   increasing by five percent after retirement.
    (b)   decreasing by five to ten percent after retirement.
    (c)   decreasing by one-third to one-half after retirement.
    (d)   increasing by thirty to forty percent after retirement.

16. According to *Bernice Neugarten* and *Karol Weinstein*, older grandparents are most likely to adopt the _____ *approach to grandparenting*.

    (a)   formal
    (b)   surrogate parent
    (c)   fun seeker
    (d)   reservoir of knowledge
    (e)   distant figure

17. Which of the following is *not* a style of grandparenting according to research by *Andrew Cherlin* and *Frank Furstenberg*?

    (a)   remote
    (b)   involved
    (c)   companionate
    (d)   removed

18. *Robert DiGiulo* described four stages that *widowed* people experience. The final stage is called:

    (a)   emergence.
    (b)   catharsis.
    (c)   encounter.
    (d)   respondance.
    (e)   transformation.

Matching

a.	sandwich generation	f.	functional age
b.	boomerang generation	g.	31
c.	ageism	h.	77
d.	social gerontology	i.	styles of grandparenting
e.	age norms	j.	stages of widowhood

1. The stereotypes and discriminatory treatment applied to the elderly. ____
2. Expectations of how one is to behave at any stage of life. ____
3. Remote, companionate, involved. ____
4. Increasing numbers of young adults remaining or returning to their parental homes. ____
5. Percentage of the elderly who live independently and own their own homes. ____
6. An individual's physical, intellectual, and social capacities and accomplishments. ____
7. Percentage of women over the age of sixty-five who live alone.
8. The study of the impact of sociocultural conditions on the process and consequences of aging. ____

189

9.   The middle-aged generation caught between the pressure from both ends of the age spectrum. _____
10.   Emergence, encounter, respondence, transformation. _____

<u>Fill-In</u>

1.   Three key factors affecting the level of *parental satisfaction* for parents with adult children living at home are _____, _____, and _____.

2.   _____ is the study of the impact of sociocultural conditions on the process and consequences of aging.

3.   _____ refer to the expectations of how one is to behave at any stage in life.

4.   _____ describes the stereotypes and discriminatory treatment applied to the elderly.

5.   _____ refers to an individual's physical, intellectual, and social capacities and accomplishments.

6.   Women have a *longevity* advantage over men. Researcher *Erdman Palmore* attributes half of this difference in longevity to _____ and the other half to _____ and _____.

7.   In 1996 *life expectancy* at birth was _____ years for white females and _____ years for white males. For African Americans the corresponding figures were _____ years and _____ years.

8.   Today, approximately _____ *percent of the aged in the U.S. own their homes.*

9.   In 1994, approximately _____ *percent of persons sixty-five years of age and older were working or looking for wrok.*

10.   *Andrew Cherlin* and *Frank Furstenberg* found three *styles of grandparenting*, including _____, _____, and _____.

11.   *Vira Kivitt's* research found that the _____ role was more central in the lives of African American men than it was for white men.

12.   According to *Robert DiGuilio*, a person in the _____ *stage of widowhood* has come to realize that death is a natural outcome of life and, although they have lost someone they loved, they can move on with their lives.

13.   In addition to the adjustments associated with bereavement and grief, *widows* are likely to confront two major problems: changes in their _____ and changes in their _____ situation.

14.   Approximately _____ *percent of the U.S. population has *no health insurance coverage.*

<u>Short-Answer</u>

1.   What are the current demographics concerning the *aged in the United States*? What are two important demographic projections regarding the aged over the next fifty years?

2.   What is meant by the term *sandwich generation*? Has your family experienced this phenomenon, or is it an issue on the horizon for your family?

3.   What is meant by the term *boomerang generation*? What are the demographics involved with this pattern in our society?

4.   What are the three *categories of the aged* identified by gerontologists? What are the general characteristics of each category?

5.   Describe the differences and similarities between the aged along lines of *race* and *ethnicity*.

6.   Describe the *living arrangements* of the aged in our society. What are the different patterns found for women and men?

7.   What does the research suggest about the relationship between *retirement* and *marital quality*?

8. What are the *benefits* and *conflicts* involved in grandparenting?
9. What are the patterns of *caregiving* among the elderly in the United States? What are the stresses involved for adult children as caregivers? What about spouses as caregivers?
10. What are the gender differences in the experience of *widowhood*?

PART VI: ANSWERS TO STUDY QUESTIONS

True-False

1.	T	(p. 405)	10.	T	(p. 412)
2.	T	(p. 406)	11.	T	(p. 413)
3.	F	(p. 408)	12.	F	(p. 416)
4.	T	(p. 409)	13.	T	(p. 420)
5.	T	(p. 409)	14.	T	(p. 422)
6.	F	(p. 411)	15.	T	(p. 422)
7.	T	(p. 411)	16.	T	(p. 423)
8.	T	(p. 411)	17.	F	(p. 426)
9.	F	(p. 412)	18.	F	(p. 427)

Multiple-Choice

1.	c	(p. 405)	10.	c	(p. 411)
2.	d	(p. 405)	11.	a	(p. 411)
3.	b	(p. 405)	12.	d	(p. 413)
4.	a	(p. 406)	13.	c	(pp. 414-415)
5.	a	(p. 406)	14.	b	(p. 415)
6.	c	(p. 407)	15.	c	(p. 416)
7.	c	(p. 408)	16.	a	(p. 419)
8.	d	(p. 409)	17.	d	(p. 419)
9.	d	(p. 410)	18.	e	(p. 426)

Matching

1.	c	(p. 407)	6.	f	(p. 408)
2.	e	(p. 407)	7.	g	(p. 411)
3.	i	(p. 419)	8.	d	(p. 407)
4.	b	(p. 406)	9.	a	(p. 405)
5.	h	(p. 412)	10.	j	(p. 426)

Fill-In

1. younger siblings, employment status, grandchildren (p. 406)
2. Social gerontology (p. 407)
3. Age norms (p. 407)
4. Ageism (p. 407)
5. Functional age (p. 408)
6. genetics, social roles, environmental factors (p. 409)
7. 79.6, 73, 74.2, 66.1 (p. 410)

8.   77 (p. 412)
9.   12 (p. 414)
10.   remote, companionate, involved (p. 419)
11.   grandfather (p. 420)
12.   emergence (p. 426)
13.   self-identity, financial (427)
14.   16 (p. 429)

PART VII: IN FOCUS—IMPORTANT ISSUES

- Characteristics of Later-Life Families

Concerning the *boomerang generation*, how do each of the following factors affect parental satisfaction?

Younger siblings:

Employment status:

Grandchildren:

What is *social gerontology*? Why is it such an increasing important field of study for our society?

- The Demographics of Aging: Defining "Old"

Briefly describe each of the following three *categories of the elderly:*

Young-old:

Middle-old:

Old-old:

Why do the authors tell us that longevity for women can be a *mixed blessing*?

Identify one important demographic pattern in our society for each of the following variables:

Race:

Ethnicity:

Social class:

- Marriages in Later Life

    How does *marital quality* and *marital happiness* tend to vary across the years of a marriage?

- Living Arrangements

    Briefly describe the living arrangements of the elderly in our society, differentiating between the patterns for women and men.

    What are the four *patterns of retirement* identified in the text? What factors most influence satisfaction in retirement for married couples?

- Intergenerational Relationships

    Briefly describe the nature and quality of contact between the elderly and their extended family members in the United States.

- Evolving Patterns of Kinship: Grandparenthood

  What are the four *interaction patterns* found among middle-class grandparents and their grandchildren? What factors do you think would be linked to each pattern?

  What are the three *styles of grandparenting*? Describe each. Which sounds most appealing to you (first as a grandchild and second as a grandparent)? Why?

  What points are the authors making about *unplanned parenting*?

- The Child-Free Elderly

  How many elderly are child-free? What are the consequences of being child-free for the elderly?

- Sibling Relationships

  What are two important demographic facts being identified by the authors about sibling relationships among the aged in our society today?

- Health and Illness

  What is meant by ADL? What are the demographic patterns concerning this measure of *health*?

What are the patterns found regarding *adult children as caregivers* for their aged parents?

What are the major *stresses of caregiving*?

- The Experience of Widowhood

  Describe each of the following *stages of widowhood*:

  Encounter

  Respondence

  Emergence

  Transformation

- Implications for Social Policy

  What are three major points made by the authors regarding social policy and the aged, particularly looking ahead to the increasing proportion of our society's population who will be elderly over the next fifty years?

PART VIII: ANALYSIS AND COMMENT

- Applying the Sociological Imagination: "Is Ageism Dead?" (p. 408)

    Key Points: Questions/Comments:

- Family Profile: "The Gottleib Family" (p. 415)

    Key Points: Questions/Comments:

- In Other Places: "The Role and Status of the Elderly: Varied and Changing" (p. 417)

    Key Points: Questions/Comments:

- Strengthening Marriages and Families: "Coping with the Caregiving Role" (p. 425)

    Key Points: Questions/Comments:

- **Writing Your Own Script: "Thinking about Later Life" (p. 428)**

    Key Points: Questions/Comments:

15 Marriages and Families In the Twenty-First Century: U.S. and World Trends

PART I: CHAPTER OUTLINE

I.   Challenges of a World Economy
II.   Inequities In Income and Wealth
III. Health and Health Care
      A.   Trends in Drug Use and Associated Health Problems
      B.   Alcohol
      C.   Addiction and the Family
IV.   Meeting the Needs of Children: Foster Care and Adoption
      A.   Problems within the Child Welfare System
      B.   Characteristics of Adoptive Parents
      C.   International Adoptions
      D.   Transracial (Interracial) Adoptions
V.   The Challenge of Racism and Ethnic Discrimination In Family Life
      A.   Racism in the United States
      B.   Racism in a Global Context
VI.   Safety and Security: Gangs, Street Violence, and Violence in America's Schools
VII. Terrorism and War
      A.   Terrorism in the United States
      B.   War
      C.   A World of Refugees
VIII. Families Coping With Loss: Dying and Death
      A.   The Process of Dying
      B.   The Needs and Tasks of the Dying
      C.   The Right-to-Die Movement
IX.   Strengthening Marriages and Families: The Ongoing Challenges of Living In a Global World
X.   Summary
XI.   Key Terms
XII. Questions for Study and Reflection
XIII. Further Reading

PART II: LEARNING OBJECTIVES

1. To become more aware of the challenges being posed by the world economy today.
2. To identify and analyze inequalities in wealth and income, both within our society and throughout the world.
3. To describe the relative health of the U.S. population as compared to other countries around the world.
4. To address the issues of inequalities in health care within our society and the increasing costs of health care.
5. To consider the trends in drug use in our society, particularly in terms of how these are related to health problems.
6. To consider issues concerning our child welfare system, particularly in terms of adoption and foster care.
7. To discuss the challenge of racism and ethnic discrimination in our society and around the world.
8. To describe the problem of street gangs in our society.
9. To define and illustrate terrorism and war.
10. To consider the worldwide problem of refugees.
11. To discuss issues relating to families coping with loss.
12. To address questions concerning the challenges of living in a global world, particularly those relevant to gender inequalities.

PART III: KEY TERMS

alcoholism

bereavement

closed adoption

disability

disenfranchised grief

drug

drug abuse

drug use

ethnic cleansing

euthanasia

fictive kin

global interdependence

grief

health

individual racism

open adoption

racism

refugee

symbolic racism

terrorism

PART IV: IMPORTANT RESEARCHERS

Lois Benjamin   Kenneth Doka

Richard Kalish   Elisabeth Kubler-Ross

Helen Lopata   Carole McKelvy and JoEllen Stevens

Joseph Shapiro

PART V: STUDY QUESTIONS

True-False

1. According to the authors, *globalization* began in 1989 with the fall of communism.   T   F
2. *Multinational corporations* are virtually always under control of only one nation.   T   F
3. The distribution of *income* in the United States is more equally distributed today than was the case in 1980.   T   F
4. *Wealth inequality* in the U.S. is greater than in any other industrial nation.   T   F
5. The U.S. has the *lowest infant mortality rate* and the *highest life expectancy* of any industrialized society in the world.   T   F
6. The rate of poverty among *disabled* people is much higher than it is among the able-bodied.   T   F

7. Early research and treatment of *alcoholism* focused on the drinking alcoholic. T F
8. The idea behind *foster care* is that substitute families will provide short-term care until the children can be adopted or returned to their biological parents. T F
9. Estimates are that about eighty percent of children currently in *foster care* in the U.S. are eligible to be adopted. T F
10. Lesbians and gays are *not legally allowed* in the U.S. to become *adoptive parents*. T F
11. Approximately forty percent of the children who are eligible for adoption in the U.S. are African American. T F
12. Violent crime in the U.S. is primarily *intraracial*. T F
13. According to the authors, the intensity and frequency of *wars* have increased in the twentieth century, and a major characteristic of contemporary war is that civilians are the primary victims. T F
14. Women and children comprise about forty percent of the world's *refugees*. T F
15. *Elisabeth Kubler-Ross* includes hope, and curiosity as two of the stages in the process of death and dying. T F
16. Research shows that in industrial societies, roughly two-thirds of women's total work burden is spent on *unpaid activities* and one-third on paid activities; for men, the shares are reversed. T F

Multiple-Choice

1.

Today, the *wealthiest fifth of the world's population* control about _____ percent of the total economic activity as measured by gross national product, domestic savings, investment, and world trade.

(a)   50
(b)   60
(c)   70
(d)   85
(e)   96

2.   The difference in pay between the typical worker and chief executive today is more than _____ to one.

(a)   100
(b)   50
(c)   25
(d)   18

3.   The *top .5 percent* of households in the United States own approximately _____ percent of the nation's *wealth*.

(a)   10
(b)   20
(c)   35
(d)   40
(e)   55

4. Approximately one-half of the *world's poor* live in:

(a) Africa.
(b) southeast Asia.
(c) South America.
(d) North America and Europe.

5. The *World Health Organization* defines *health* as:

(a) the absence of illness.
(b) a state of complete physical, mental, and social well-being.
(c) the absence of mortality.
(d) longevity equal to or exceeding the life expectancy for a particular population.
(e) functional equivalence.

6. Approximately _____ percent of our nation's citizens do not have any *health insurance.*

(a) 4
(b) 10
(c) 16
(d) 35

7. The most commonly used illicit drug in the U.S. today is:

(a) heroin.
(b) cocaine.
(c) marijuana.
(d) inhalants.

8. The problems within the *child-welfare system* are many and varied, including:

(a) welfare workers continue to turn over at a high rate.
(b) the pool of foster families is shrinking.
(c) the needs of children in care are becoming increasingly complex.
(d) all of the above.
(e) none of the above.

9. What percentage of children in the U.S. each year are *born into poverty?*

(a) 10
(b) 25
(c) 15
(d) 20

10. Which of the following is/are accurate concerning *adoptions*?

   (a)   approximately twenty-five percent of the adoptions of children with special needs are by single women and men; five percent of other adoptions are by single people
   (b)   private adoptions may be open or closed
   (c)   couples who adopt are most commonly white and affluent; with at least some college education
   (d)   it has only been recently that lesbians and gays have been allowed to become adoptive parents
   (e)   all of the above are accurate

11. The denial of the presence of racial inequality in society and the opposition to any social policy aimed at undoing the effects of racism and discrimination refers to:

   (a)   institutional racism
   (b)   structural prejudice
   (c)   cultural discrimination
   (d)   symbolic racism

12. Some experts estimate that *gangs* account for as much as _____ percent of crime and violence in this country.

   (a)   40
   (b)   30
   (c)   60
   (d)   90
   (e)   10

13. Every _____ *hours* in this country a child or adolescent uses a handgun to en her or his own life.

   (a)   24
   (b)   18
   (c)   12
   (d)   6
   (e)   2

14. Which of the following is the *first stage* in *Elisabeth Kubler-Ross'* process of death and dying?

   (a)   anger
   (b)   denial
   (c)   depression
   (d)   bargaining

15. The 1976 landmark case of *Karen Ann Quinlan* gave public recognition to:

   (a)   the debate over the right to die.
   (b)   the issue of privacy in adoptions.
   (c)   the devaluation of children.
   (d)   the problem of welfare dependency.

Matching

a.	global interdependence	**g.**	symbolic racism
b.	health	**h.**	ethnic cleansing
c.	disability	**i.**	terrorism
d.	narcotics	**j.**	refugees
e.	stimulants	**k.**	bereavement
f.	racism	**l.**	disenfranchised grief

1. An ideology of domination and a set of social, economic, and political practices by which one or more groups define themselves as superior and other groups as inferior and they systematically deny the latter groups full access and anticipation in mainstream society. ____
2. Opium, morphine, heroin. ____
3. Circumstances in which a person experiences a sense of loss but does not have a socially recognized right, role, or capacity to grieve. ____
4. A physical or health condition that stigmatizes or causes discrimination. ____
5. The denial of the presence of racial inequality in society and the opposition to any social policy aimed at undoing the effects of racism and discrimination. ____
6. A state in which the lives of people around the word are intertwined closely and in which any one nation's problems increasingly cut across cultural and geographic boundaries. ____
7. The state of being deprived of a loved one by death. ____
8. People who leave their country because of a "well-founded fear" of persecution for reasons of race, religion, nationality, social group, or political opinion. ____
9. Cocaine, crack, tobacco. ____
10. A systematic campaign by which one category of people tries to rid a region of others who are different in some significant way. ____
11. The employment or threat of violence, fear, or intimidation by individuals or groups as a political or revolutionary strategy to achieve political goals. ____
12. A state of complete physical, emotional, and social well-being. ____

Fill-In

1. _____ refers to a state in which the lives of people around the world are intertwined closely and in which any one nation's problems increasingly cut across cultural and geographic boundaries.
2. The *poorest fifth* of the world's population control about _____ percent of the world's economic activity.
3. Approximately one-half of the world's poor live in _____ and about one-third live in _____.
4. _____ is defined by the World Health Organization as a state of complete physical, mental, and social well-being.
5. Two commonly used indicators of well-being focused on in this chapter to compare the relative health of nations are _____ and _____.
6. According to some reports, _____ percent of the U.S. population is *disabled*.
7. In the United States, 86.2 percent of the population with no disability is employed, compared with only _____ percent of those with a disability.

8.   The most commonly used and abused drugs are _____, _____, _____, _____, _____, and _____.

9.   Alcohol is responsible for about _____ deaths per year.

10. The _____ code (circa 1758 B.C. in Babylon), contained laws regulating the operation and management of drinking establishments.

11. _____ is an ideology of domination and a set of social, economic, and political practices by which one or more groups define themselves as superior and other groups as inferior and then systematically deny the latter groups full access and participation in mainstream society.

12. The *murder rate* in the U.S. is _____ times that of Northern Ireland, _____ times higher than England, and _____ times higher than Japan.

13. Among African American males between the ages of 15 and 24 the leading cause of death is _____.

14. Americans are the target of *terrorism* worldwide in one in _____ cases.

15. Regarding the problem of *refugees* around the world, according to some sources one in _____ people worldwide has been forced into flight.

16. _____ refers to the state of being deprived of a loved one by death, whereas _____ is the emotional response to this loss.

17. *Suicide* is the _____ leading cause of death in the United States.

18. The term _____ derives from the Greek words meaning "good death," or dying without pain or suffering.

19. *Euthanasia* can take two forms: _____ in which medical treatment is terminated, and _____ which refers to actions deliberately taken to end a person's life.

20. A clear example that women are denied full participation in societies around the world is that of the 900 million people who are *illiterate* in the world, women outnumber men _____ to one.

Short-Answer

1.   What are the major indicators that a *global economy* exists?

2.   What is the evidence that there is inequality in *wealth* and *income* in the United States?

3.   How is *health* defined by the World Health Organization? What is your opinion of this definition? What is the evidence that there is global inequality in health?

4.   What are the problems within the *child welfare system* operating in the United States in terms of adoption and foster care policies and programs?

5.   Differentiate between the concepts of *drug use* and *drug abuse*?

6.   How serious a problem are *gangs* in the United States? What is the evidence being presented in this chapter concerning gang violence and criminal behavior?

7.   What points are the authors making concerning the civil atrocities of *war*?

8.   According to *Helen Lopata*, what are the four tasks for successful grief resolution?

9.   Differentiate between the concepts of *grief* and *disenfranchised grief*.

10. According to *Elisabeth Kubler-Ross*, what are the *stages of dying*? What are the criticisms of this model?

11. What are the points being made by the authors concerning *civilian causalities of war*? What is the evidence being presented?

12. What are the controversies involved in the *right-to-die movement*? What are your opinions on this subject?
13. What is the evidence that *racism* is a powerful force in the U.S. today?
14. What do our authors tell us about *global racism*?

PART VI: ANSWERS TO STUDY QUESTIONS

True-False

1.	F	(p. 432)	9.	F	(pp. 443-444)
2.	F	(p. 433)	10.	F	(p. 445)
3.	F	(p. 434)	11.	T	(p. 446)
4.	T	(p. 435)	12.	T	(p. 451)
5.	F	(p. 435)	13.	T	(p. 456)
6.	T	(p. 437)	14.	F	(p. 457)
7.	T	(p. 442)	15.	F	(p. 459)
8.	T	(p. 443)	16.	T	(p. 462)

Multiple-Choice

1.	d	(p. 433)	9.	b	(p. 444)
2.	a	(p. 434)	10.	e	(p. 445)
3.	c	(p. 434)	11.	d	(p. 459)
4.	b	(p. 435)	12.	a	(p. 450)
5.	b	(p. 435)	13.	e	(p. 452)
6.	c	(p. 439)	14.	b	(p. 459)
7.	c	(p. 440)	15.	a	(p. 462)
8.	d	(p. 443)			

Matching

1.	f	(p. 447)	7.	k	(p. 460)
2.	d	(p. 440)	8.	j	(p. 457)
3.	l	(p. 461)	9.	e	(p. 440)
4.	c	(p. 437)	10.	h	(p. 450)
5.	g	(p. 449)	11.	i	(p. 455)
6.	a	(p. 432)	12.	b	(p. 435)

Fill-In

1. Global interdependence (p. 432)
2. 1 (p. 433)
3. southeast Asia, Africa (p. 433)
4. Health (p. 435)
5. life expectancy, infant mortality (p. 435)
6. 19 (p. 437)
7. 13.8 (p. 438)

8.   narcotics, depressants, stimulants, hallucinogens, cannabis, organic solvents (p. 440)
9.   200,000 (p. 441)
10.   Hammurabi (p. 441)
11.   Racism (p. 447)
12.   2, 9, 11 (p. 451)
13.   homicide (p. 452)
14.   four (p. 455)
15.   115 (p. 457)
16.   Bereavement, grief (p. 460)
17.   ninth (p. 461)
18.   euthanasia (p. 462)
19.   passive, active (p. 462)
20.   two (p. 462)

PART VII: IN FOCUS--IMPORTANT ISSUES

- Challenges of a World Economy

  What are five *indicators* identified by the authors concerning the consequences of the *new international division of labor* for families?

- Inequities In Income and Wealth

  Provide two pieces of evidence to suggest there is *inequality* in income and wealth in the United States:

- Health and Health Care

  What are three major *indicators of well-being* used to compare a society's relative health to other nations? How does the U.S. compare on these measures to other industrialized societies?

  How does the U.S. differ from other industrialized nations in terms of *health insurance coverage*?

What are the five most commonly used and abused drugs in the United States? Provide an example for each type and indicators that each is being abused in our society.

- Meeting the Needs of Children: Foster Care and Adoption

  What are five major *problems within the child welfare system*?

- The Challenge of Racism and Ethnic Discrimination In Family Life

  Provide an example in our society for each of the following: *racism, individual racism, symbolic racism*:

- Safety and Security: Gangs, Street Violence, and Violence in America's Schools

  What are four major points being made by the authors concerning *gang violence* and *street violence* in our society?

- Terrorism and War

  What is one important fact about *terrorism* you learned by reading this section of the chapter?

  In a paragraph describe the effects of *war* on civilian populations, especially women.

- Families Coping With Loss: Dying and Death

  What are the five stages through which Elizabeth Kubler-Ross believes a dying patient goes through?

  How does the *suicide rate* in the U.S. compare to other industrialized societies?

- Strengthening Marriages and Families: The Ongoing Challenges of Living In a Global World

  What is the evidence that women are experiencing inequality on a global scale?

  What policy recommendations are being supported by our authors to strengthen marriages and families worldwide?

PART VIII: ANALYSIS AND COMMENT

- Searching the Internet: "Women and Disabilities: Ontario, Canada" (p. 438)

  Key Points: Questions/Comments:

- Searching the Internet: "Key Facts about American Children" (p. 444)

    Key Points: Questions/Comments:

- Social Policy Issues: "Legislating Parental Responsibility: Are Parents to Blame for Their Children's Violent Behavior?" (p. 454)

    Key Points: Questions/Comments:

- Family Profile: "Fawzia and Michael Boctor" (p. 458)

    Key Points: Questions/Comments:

- Social Policy Issues: "The Debate Over Physician-Assisted Suicide" (p. 463)

    Key Points: Questions/Comments:

- Writing Your Own Script: "Thinking Critically" (p. 464)

  Key Points: Questions/Comments:

Notes

Notes

Notes

Notes